MARTIN
SPEAKS OUT ON
THE CULTS

MARTIN
SPEAKS OUT ON
THE CULTS

DR. WALTER MARTIN

Regal Books

A Division of GL Publications
Ventura, California, U.S.A.

Published by Regal Books
A Division of GL Publications
Ventura, California 93006
Printed in U.S.A.

Library of Congress Cataloging in Publication Data.

Martin, Walter Ralston, 1928-
    Martin speaks out on the cults.

    Bibliography: p.
    1. Cults—Controversial literature.   2. Christian
sects—Controversial literature.   3. Occult sciences—
Controversial literature.   I. Title.
BL80.2.M2894   1983   291   83-12368
ISBN 0-88449-103-X

3 4 5 6 7 8 9 / 91 90 89 88 87

Rights for publishing this book in other languages are contracted by Gospel Literature International (GLINT) foundation. GLINT also provides technical help for the adaptation, translation, and publishing of Bible study resources and books in scores of languages worldwide. For further information, contact GLINT, Post Office Box 488, Rosemead, California, 91770, U.S.A., or the publisher.

CONTENTS

Acknowledgments

In the years of development that this small volume has undergone, many people contributed to produce the present form. First, thanks should go to Shelton College, First Baptist Bible School, and the periodicals *Eternity, Our Hope,* and *The Examiner,* by means of which some of this material was first delivered to the public as lectures and articles. Other important information is from my film series, "Martin Speaks Out on the Cults," and my thanks go to Vision House and its editorial staff for help in presenting that material here.

I wish to express my thanks to Dr. Frank E. Gaebelein, former headmaster of the Stony Brook School, for his patient and constructive criticisms of this work; to the late Dr. Donald Grey Barnhouse for his help through the pages of *Eternity* Magazine; and to Mr. Russell Hitt, former editor of *Eternity,* for his many fine suggestions, corrections, and useful literary assists.

My thanks also to Dr. E. Schuyler English for his support and to Rev. Gilbert Peterson for his editorial assistance. I would like to thank researchers Clark F. Hyman and Bryce Pettit for their work on the chapters on Mormonism and Armstrongism and researcher and writer Mrs. Gretchen Passantino for her efforts in helping me to update, revise, and edit the last three editions of this book.

Preface

Since 1955, when this work first appeared under the title *The Rise of the Cults,* much theological water has gone under the bridge of history. The cults and the occult were even then surging toward their great growth and tidal wave of propaganda that today, twenty-eight years later, crests high on the ramparts of the Christian Church. Fortunately, by the grace of God, I was privileged to foresee that this deluge was coming, and I sought to warn the Church that we must be prepared to meet and resist the rise of the cults and the occult, while never forgetting the task of evangelizing those caught within their webs of deception. History and experience tell us that the two-fold ministry of the Church—evangelism and the defense of the gospel—can be effectively realized and implemented.

Unfortunately and to my sorrow, that warning went largely unheeded, and I was described as an "alarmist." The public was told that the cults were not outpacing the Church. However, this was not the case, as any student of the last decade well knows. Today a virulent cultic and occultic revival is sweeping our country, dating from approximately 1965; much of the world has now begun to feel its powerful impact. But there is a real ray of hope in this dark picture: the Lord has begun to arouse His people.

Thinking Christians now realize that the danger to them, their children, and their grandchildren is real, not imagined. They have also become aware that cultists and occultists can be successfully answered and evangelized, thus turning enemies of the gospel into stalwart Christians. I have never regretted being right about anything quite so much in my entire ministry. I wish it had been otherwise; I wish that just preaching the gospel without defending the faith effectively and evangelizing the cults directly would have contained the rise of the cults. But the contrary facts are before us on every side. The cults simply will not go away, and neither can they any longer be ignored or drowned in a sea of evasive rhetoric, statistics, or argument. The rise of the cults is upon us with a vengeance, at home and on every major world mission field.

The response of the church must be immediate and positive if this rise is to be checked and perhaps contained, though this now will take an act of sovereign grace because of the enormous multiplication and proliferation of cultic structures. The time for talk is over; the time for *action* in the name of the gospel has arrived. In a word, the challenge is here, the time is *now*.

This introduction to the cults, *Martin Speaks Out on the Cults*, has, by the grace of God, become part of the action for evangelizing cultists which is so sorely needed. In its previous editions it has been used by earnest Christians to equip them to share their faith effectively with cultists and to win those lost souls for the Kingdom of God. Cultists have read this book in other editions and its challenge has driven them to investigate the claims of the true Jesus Christ of the Bible and to abandon the false Christs of the cults. With the addition of important and current information (adapted from my video series of the same title) this new edition will, with God's help, continue the fight against error and for the One who is the only Way, Truth, and Life, Jesus Christ our Lord.

Walter Martin
San Juan Capistrano
California, 1983

A COMMENDATION

from
the late Dr. Wilbur M. Smith

Apart from sheer unbelief and the deep paganism of our modern civilization, the greatest hindrance to an acceptance of the saving gospel of Jesus Christ is the teaching of these false cults, which, on the periphery of Christianity, deceivingly and inaccurately use many of the sacred terms of the true Christian faith. These cults are spreading with phenomenal speed, and by them millions are being led astray. The world as such, of course, can never be expected to expose the evil roots and false teachings of these religions—this can be expected only from those who know the Word of God and the truth as it is in Christ. The danger is that too many in the church, unacquainted with and really uninterested in the history and actual teachings of these groups, are lulled into a state of indifference toward them, or, even worse, into believing that these false religions are also a true way to God, whereas they lead to nothing else but eternal death.

No man in America today has carried on such extended, careful research in this important area of contemporary religious life as has Dr. Walter Martin. After collaborating with Norman Klann on a number of articles and two excellent volumes, *Jehovah of the Watchtower* and *The Christian Science Myth,* Dr. Martin has brought together the results of his years of study in this comprehensive work, *The Rise of the Cults.* * This is the most significant work on cults to appear in this country in the last twenty years, and it is certainly the only one that is up-to-date now.

* former title

one
The Rise of the Cults

Thirty million people in the United States today pledge allegiance to one of the thousands of cults proliferating in our relativistic, pluralistic society. Thirty million people think they are following the true gospel, the true religion, the true Jesus. But they're not. They have been deceived by Satan, the "God of this world," who delights in tricking people into serving him in the name of religion. Why this great deception? Why the millions of people who are so thirsty for something to believe in that they will cling to any cult that comes along? Jesus Christ talked about this very phenomenon and how it would sweep the land in this, the "last days."

In Matthew 24, the disciples asked Jesus what it would be like at the very end, just before His Second Coming. They said, "Tell us, when shall these things be?

and what shall be the sign of thy coming, and of the end of the world?" (Matt. 24:3). Jesus gave them a lengthy answer designed to keep Christians from being deceived. He answered them with "Take heed that no man deceive you. For many shall come in my name, saying, I am Christ; and shall deceive many" (vv. 4-5). Note that the very first "sign" is that false Christs will arise and will be able to deceive many.

The proliferation of the cults around the world today is indicative of the fight Satan is putting up as he sees his imminent demise. In fact, Jesus Christ four times in this one chapter of Matthew warns of the coming deceptions: (1) "For many shall come in my name, saying, I am Christ; and shall deceive many" (v. 5); (2) "And many false prophets shall rise, and shall deceive many" (v. 11); (3) "Then if any man shall say unto you, Lo, here is Christ, or there; believe it not. For there shall arise false Christs, and false prophets, and shall shew great signs and wonders; insomuch that, if it were possible, they shall deceive the very elect" (vv. 23-24); (4) "Wherefore if they shall say unto you, Behold, he is in the desert; go not forth: behold, he is in the secret chambers; believe it not. For as the lightning cometh out of the east, and shineth even unto the west; so shall also the coming of the Son of man be" (v. 26-27).

We are told to beware of false Christs, to beware of false prophets, and to beware of false teachers. How do these agents of Satan operate? In Matthew 7:15-23 we have an example: the false teachers are able to use the name of Jesus Christ and even to perform wonderful works in His name. And yet, at the end, their deceit and their evil goals will be revealed and Jesus Christ the Judge will declare, "I never knew you: depart from me, ye that work iniquity" (v. 23).

We should not be dismayed by this talk of deception

and false teaching. Our Lord has given us remedies for the wiles of the devil and his agents. With submission to the Lordship of Jesus Christ, diligence in studying the Word of God, and hearts open to sharing the gospel of our Lord with those who are lost, we can be part of Christ's triumph over Satan. This handbook (and my related video series, also called "Martin Speaks Out on the Cults") can help to equip you in studying the Word of God as part of your reaching out in love to those snared in the cults.

In this book we will review the rise of the Cults, the Jehovah's Witnesses (the Watchtower Bible and Tract Society), the Mormons (the Church of Jesus Christ of Latter-day Saints), the mind sciences (including Christian Science and Unity School of Christianity), the world of the occult (including Spiritism), and the new cults (including the Unification Church—Moonies, the Hare Krishnas, etc.).

Perhaps it is best to begin our study of these cults by defining precisely what we mean when we attach the label of *cult* to a particular organization, so that as we progress into the field we shall not be hampered by the problem of fluctuating terminology.

Today on the mission fields of the world, and indeed on every street corner of the major cities of the six continents, cultism is on the march.

By cultism we mean the adherence to major doctrines which are pointedly contradictory to orthodox Christianity, yet which claim the distinction of either tracing their origin to orthodox sources or of being in essential harmony with those sources. Cultism, in short, *is any major deviation from orthodox Christianity relative to the cardinal doctrines of the Christian faith.*

A cult, then, is a group of people polarized around someone's interpretation of the Bible and is characterized by major deviations from orthodox Christianity relative to the cardinal doctrines of the Christian faith, particularly the fact that God became man in Jesus Christ. Thus we see the Mormons polarized around Joseph Smith and Brigham Young, Christian Scientists around Mary Baker Eddy, and the other groups around their respective leaders.

The cults say they believe in Jesus Christ. Which Jesus? Each cult has its own version of the identity of Jesus Christ. On one thing their teachings are all the same: they all teach a different Jesus from the one revealed in Holy Scripture, a false Christ, a counterfeit of the Lord of Glory. The Jesus of the Jehovah's Witnesses is Michael the Archangel, first and mightiest creation of Jehovah God. The Jesus of the Mormons is the spirit-brother of Lucifer, the product of sexual union between Mary and the Holy Spirit, one of many gods. The Jesus of the mind sciences is not Christ but a man manifesting the divine Christ principle. The Jesus of the occult was a master wizard, or an incarnation of some cosmic consciousness, or a spiritually superior reincarnated individual.

Among all of the myriad Jesuses promulgated by the thousands of cults, none is the Jesus Christ of the Bible. Second Corinthians 11:3-4, 13-15 affirms that there are false Christs and even false Holy Spirits and false gospels: "But I fear, lest by any means, as the serpent beguiled Eve through his subtilty, so your minds should be corrupted from the simplicity that is in Christ. For if he that cometh preacheth another Jesus, whom we have not preached, or if ye receive another spirit, which ye have not received, or another gospel, which ye have not accepted, ye might well bear with him . . . . For such are false apostles, deceitful workers, transforming themselves into the apostles of Christ. And no marvel; for

Satan himself is transformed into an angel of light. Therefore it is no great thing if his ministers also be transformed as the ministers of righteousness; whose end shall be according to their works."

Prominent among the cults are Jehovah's Witnesses, Mormons, the mind sciences (Christian Science, Unity School of Christianity, Science of Mind, etc.), those cults with occultic alliances (Spiritism, Religious Science, Church of Satan, etc.), and the new cults (Moonies, Hare Krishnas, Children of God, etc.). All of these deny both the biblical doctrines of the Trinity and the deity of Jesus Christ. Numerically, the thousands of cults represented in America alone have a following exceeding thirty million persons, as well as missionary programs which circle the globe in ever-increasing numbers. Jehovah's Witnesses alone boast over one hundred thousand "pioneers" (like missionaries), and at one of their International Conventions held in New York City's Yankee Stadium, the zealous Witnesses filled both the Stadium (eighty-five thousand) and the neighboring Polo Grounds (fifty thousand) to overflowing. Beyond this astonishing and alarming fact, Jehovah's Witnesses have around forty thousand congregations circulating their literature in 160 languages and 270 lands, denying from pole to pole the Trinity and the deity of Jesus Christ, His physical resurrection and visible return to judge the world.

Christian Science, one of the mind sciences, on the other hand, has concentrated on reaching the larger centers of world population; few indeed are those cities where Christian Science churches and reading rooms are not conspicuous. Through the excellent propaganda efforts of their three chief publications, the *Christian Science Monitor, Sentinel,* and *Journal,* the Christian Science religion has managed to gain for itself a position and reputation that Mrs. Eddy was completely incapable of endowing it with, and has won acceptance among many uninformed sources as a nominally Christian religion. However, nothing could be further from the truth of the matter, for in reality Christian Science denies virtually every cardinal doctrine of the Christian faith, not only those previously mentioned, but many others far too numerous to record in this overview chapter.

The combined memberships of the various mind science cults throughout the United States is somewhere over four million persons. Whereas Jehovah's Witnesses are for the most part outwardly respectful of biblical authority, the mind scientists deny the absolute authority of the Scriptures outright and are not in the least disturbed by the implications of their attitude.[1]

In contrast to both Jehovah's Witnesses and the mind science cults, the Church of Jesus Christ of Latter-day Saints, or the Mormons, has incorporated the prime traits of the others, emphasizing both metropolitan and rural propaganda work in a renewed attempt to rout evangelical Christianity from world mission fields regardless of location. From their focal point of distribution in Salt Lake City, the eager disciples of Joseph Smith and Brigham Young have increasingly widened their sphere of missionary influence. The several new temples around the world, including the recently built $15 million Mormon Temple erected in Seattle, Washington, and the various Mormon wards springing up all over the United States, bear pointed testimony to the rapid rise of the Latter-day Saints. Mormonism (as with all the previously mentioned cults) capitalizes upon the reverence most people have for the Bible, a reverence not always based upon what lies within the seldom-opened covers.

Many well-meaning persons have that peculiar kind of faith which parallels that of the man who buried a box of fruit for the winter in the belief that the frost would preserve it. He loudly insisted that his was the best fruit in the country, but upon digging it up in the spring he found it rotten and spoiled by the rigorous climatic changes of the season. Likewise, many people bury their faith, firmly insisting that it is sound, yet never bothering to dig it up or examine it to see if it has been affected by the conditions and demands of life. It is upon this type of person that cultism feeds, devouring in ever-increasing numbers those who are not sure what they believe or why they believe it.

Another of the mind science cults, the Unity School of Christianity, promotes the same "cure-alls" offered by Christian Science. In the same theological camp as Mrs. Eddy, Unity's founders, Charles and Myrtle Fillmore, sought physical health and monetary remuneration, both of which they obtained by convincing over three million persons that "sickness" and "death" are illusions, and that the bodily resurrection and the deity of our Lord are unnecessary doctrines.[2] Negating, as it does, the authority of the Bible, and spiritualizing whatever texts are found to be embarrassing, Unity, like Christian Science, has built a multimillion-dollar business upon the false premises that God is impersonal, that sin and sickness are largely illusory, and that Unity is the true Christian religion. The mind science cults, as much as all the rest of the cults here discussed, represent the false teachings, the cheap imitations of the truth, spoken of in 1 John 4:1-3:

"Beloved, believe not every spirit, but try the spirits whether they are of God: because many false prophets are gone out into the world. Hereby know ye the Spirit of God: Every spirit that confesseth that Jesus Christ is come in the flesh is of God: And every spirit that confesseth not that Jesus Christ is come in the flesh is not of

God: and this is that spirit of antichrist, whereof ye have heard that it should come; and even now already is it in the world."

When surveying these problems, therefore, it is vitally essential that we understand one of the basic causes of cultism: *the unfortunate failure of the church to insti-tute and emphasize a definite, systematic plan for cult evangelism and apologetics.* The average Christian is, sad to say, terribly unprepared to defend his faith thor-oughly. In a word, he knows *what* he believes, but too often he does not know *why.* This is the chink in the armor of orthodoxy into which the cults have driven a subtle wedge, and through which innumerable false doc-trines have penetrated with alarming rapidity and telling effect.

One of the weakest spots in the Church's defense against heresy and apostasy is the common belief that to disagree with anyone is always wrong. The line goes, "Sure, the Mormons may be wrong about there being many gods, but if I tell that to my Mormon neighbor, she'll be offended and never talk to me again. I just can't hurt her feelings like that!" With courtesy like that, the Mormon neighbor is being cheated out of hearing the glorious news of the gospel and the truth which is *only* in Christ Jesus our Lord! There is no room for rudeness in preaching the gospel; neither is there room for deceit or holding back of the truth. Yes, some cultists will be offended by any disagreement on a Christian's part. But when the truth is shared in love and with the cultist's eternal destiny in view, it cuts quickly through the jungle of cultic entrapment and allows the light of the gospel to shine on the hearts of those cultists who earnestly yearn after the truth.

The New Testament tells us that Jesus is the *only* Way, the *only* Truth, and the *only* Life. That does not change just because we Christians aren't willing to risk disturbing our own comfort to bring someone else into the kingdom! We have a mandate from the Lord Jesus Christ to share the good news truthfully and fully with those we meet. We cannot afford to allow cultists to go to hell because we are concerned about the truth "hurting their feelings." Acts 4:12 reminds us, "Neither is there salvation in any other: for there is none other name under heaven given among men, whereby we must be saved."

It is also helpful to remember, when dealing with cults, that whatever variety one may encounter, *cults are always built, not upon what the Bible teaches, but upon what the founders of the respective cults say the Bible teaches.* So in the final analysis it is necessary to refute the claims of the cult founders in order to effectively undermine faith in the related cult.

Cultism thrives principally upon two factors: *ignorance* and *uncertainty.* Where these most abound, there cultism will also be found in force. The cults consistently appeal to "reason" and "rationality," which many times they use as their sole guide in evaluating the character of God and His revelation. Hell is "unreasonable," eternal punishment is "irrational," consciousness after death is a "pagan theory," and therefore these doctrines could not be true, argue the cults, apparently oblivious to the fact that they are circumscribing the infinite God to the scope of their finite reasoning processes and imputing to Him their manifestly feeble powers of logical thought.

Most cult adherents assume God to be what they believe He should be, but Scripture tells us repeatedly that He is not to be measured by our limited abilities, but by what He has declared in His Word (Isa. 55:8; Rom. 11:33-36). The rise of the cults is therefore directly proportional to the fluctuating emphasis which the Christian

Church has placed on the teaching of biblical doctrine to Christian laymen. To be sure, a few pastors, teachers, and evangelists defend adequately their beliefs, but most of them and most of the average Christian laymen are hard put to confront and refute a well-trained cultist of almost any variety.

The shock troops of cultism are surprise and confusion. Cultists surprise the Christian by apparent mastery of his own textbook, the Bible, and confuse him with glib quotations, usually completely out of context, which appear to challenge the most cherished of orthodox tenets. " 'My Father is greater than I' (John 14:28) proves that Jesus was not God," says the self-assured Jehovah's Witness; "God is Love—how can He punish us?" echoes the Christian Scientist. The cultists maintain that all these statements are strongly supported by various Scripture verses—quoted mostly out of context and thoroughly mystifying to many concerned but unprepared Christians.

Keeping pace with the rapid rise of cult propaganda in written form has been the cultists' use of the media of television and radio, as particularly displayed in the activities of the Mormons, the mind sciences, and Jehovah's Witnesses. The Mormons spend millions of dollars in public relations activities, including, for example, their popular tourist attraction (the Polynesian Cultural Center) in Hawaii and extensive glossy advertising supplements in local, regional, and national publications. The mind science cults often concentrate their advertising dollars on religious television programming, many times presenting daily and weekly "inspirational programs," and even presenting television "specials" promoting their own particular brands of mind science teachings. The Jehovah's Witnesses are familiar to almost every American who has seen them countless times standing on busy street corners, holding up their Watchtower publications, hoping to entice passersby into reading their materials. However, this religious and promotional zeal is no substitute for correct doctrine. Unfortunately, in the recent past, if a cult "sounded" orthodox, most Christians never took the trouble to investigate it; rather, they tended to ignore it, and in so doing encouraged its expansion, a fact which today the Church most openly deplore.

Just how can this problem be solved effectively? I discuss this in chapter 7, but we should never forget that the growth of cults is a true sign of the end of the age, when "deceivers shall grow worse and worse, deceived and being deceived" (see 2 Tim. 3:13). In the following pages we will discuss some of these "last days" cults. We will see the strong power of the Enemy in leading millions of innocent people into false teaching. The faith offered by Satan through the cults is an empty faith that can never satisfy the soul. With cult after cult, we see the same characteristics which entice converts and then fail to fulfill them.

We will see the common characteristics of the cults outlined in the following pages. We will see that cults (1) are exclusivistic; (2) are blinding their followers to the truth; (3) cast fear into the hearts of their followers with threats of an imminent Armageddon (which, however, never comes when the cults predict it will); (4) promise instant spiritual, emotional, and material help and then fail to deliver; (5) brag of their exclusive "divine" revelations; (6) claim extra-biblical authority; (7) demand the followers' complete obedience to the leaders; (8) redefine all of the standard terms used to describe biblical truth, thereby effectively insulating their followers from actually understanding any biblical truth they may read; and (9) effectively alienate themselves and their followers from the rest of the world and, more importantly, from a vital and saving relationship with the Lord Jesus Christ.

We are being called today to believe in the urgency of the second coming of Christ, and we are constantly reminded of Israel and other current events in the light of biblical prophecy. We must direct our attention, then, to the fact that Jesus Christ gave the ultimate sign. That ultimate sign is the proliferation of cult teaching and cult doctrine. Let us therefore as ambassadors of Christ "put on the whole armour of God ... for we wrestle not against flesh and blood, but against principalities, against powers, against the rulers of the darkness of this world, against spiritual wickedness in high places" (Eph. 6:11-12). God grant that now in this hour of decision we may be "strong in the Lord, and in the power of His might."

NOTES

1. See Christian Science, for example, Mary Baker Eddy, ed., *Science and Health with Key to the Scriptures,* 1971, p. 139.
2. See chapter 4 of this book.

two
Jehovah's Witnesses

The first verse of the first chapter of John's Gospel is a watershed of biblical theology. One's interpretation and confession of this verse demarcates whether one is orthodox or heretical, Christian or cultic. Reliable and accurate translations of John 1:1-3, 14-18 read much like the King James Version: "In the beginning was the Word, and the Word was with God, and the Word was God. The same was in the beginning with God. All things were made by him; and without him was not any thing made that was made .... And the Word was made flesh, and dwelt among us, (and we beheld his glory, the glory as of the only begotten of the Father,) full of grace and truth. John bare witness of him, and cried, saying, This was he of whom I spake, He that cometh after me is preferred before me: for he was before me.

And of his fulness have all we received, and grace for grace. For the law was given by Moses, but grace and truth came by Jesus Christ. No man hath seen God at any time; the only begotten Son, which is in the bosom of the Father, he hath declared him."

The Gospel of John, indeed the whole Scripture— Old and New Testaments, affirms the absolute and full deity of our Lord Jesus Christ. He is Jehovah God ("the Word was God") and yet his Person is distinct from that of the Father ("the Word was *with* God"). In John 1:1 we see a declaration of the deity of Christ and the assumption of the doctrine of the Trinity, which we will discuss below. One of the characteristics of the cults is that they consistently deny the deity of Christ. This is true of the Jehovah's Witnesses (officially members of the Watchtower Bible and Tract Society). The Jehovah's Witnesses deny absolutely the deity of Christ. They believe that He is a creature, created by Jehovah God (only the Father is Jehovah) before any of the *rest* of His creation. How do the Jehovah's Witnesses deal with the clear declaration of John 1:1? Their only recourse is to change God's Word through mistranslation, as they do in their own "translation" of the Bible, *The New World Translation of the Holy Scriptures*. "In [the] beginning the Word was, and the Word was with God, and the Word was a god."[1]

There is not a shred of grammatical, textual, or historical evidence in support of such a mistranslation. It is a deliberate attempt on the part of the Society to deny our Lord the honor and worship to which He is entitled. Jesus Christ is not "a god": He is our "Lord and God," as the Apostle Thomas affirmed (John 20:28). We shall examine this unbiblical doctrine and poor translation further below.[2] It suffices now for us to know that this one false doctrine alone is enough to place the Jehovah's Witness organization outside the Christian Church and in the world of the cults. However, we shall see that the Watchtower teaches many other false doctrines as well, including salvation by works, denial of the personality and deity of the Holy Spirit, and denial of the bodily resurrection and visible Second Coming of our Lord Jesus Christ.

The Jehovah's Witnesses today are a very real threat to the Christian Church. From just thirty members in 1874 the Watchtower has grown to over four million members (1981) worldwide. The first edition of *Zion's Watch Tower* was six thousand copies per month; today *The Watchtower,* its great grandchild, distributes twenty-three million copies per month in seventy-eight languages worldwide! Its partner magazine *Awake* has a current worldwide circulation of over eighteen million in sixty-seven languages! The Watchtower organization is represented by branches in more than 225 countries around the world. What is the history of the Watchtower Bible and Tract Society and what is its theology?

THE HISTORY OF THE *WATCHTOWER*

On February 16, 1852, in the state of Pennsylvania, just outside Pittsburgh, a son was born to Joseph L. Russell and his wife, Anna Eliza, and was subsequently christened Charles Taze Russell. Young Russell spent most of his boyhood in the area known as Allegheny, a suburb of Pittsburgh, where at the age of twenty-five he had become a successful businessman. Charles Russell was a Congregationalist by denomination and, from what is known of his early history, a zealous but poorly educated student of the Bible. It was as a direct result of his interest in biblical things that Russell in 1870 organized a Bible study group, which in 1876 elected him "pastor." By this time "Pastor" Russell had totally rejected many of the cardinal doctrines of historic Christianity, such as the

Trinity, the deity of Christ, Christ's physical resurrection and return, and the doctrine of eternal retribution for sin.

In 1879 "Pastor" Russell invested some of his hard-earned savings in a small magazine, *The Herald of the Morning,* which in later years became *The Watchtower Announcing Jehovah's Kingdom* (now the official organ of Jehovah's Witnesses). Russell followed this move by forming Zion's Watch Tower Tract Society in 1884 (later The Watchtower Bible and Tract Society), which in 1886 published the first in a series of seven books (Russell wrote six of them) entitled *The Millennial Dawn.* This title was later changed to *Studies in the Scriptures,* owing to the concentrated criticisms of the Christian clergy against the Millennial Dawn movement.

In 1908 "Pastor" Russell moved his headquarters to Brooklyn, New York where a huge printing operation was undertaken. After seventy-three years of activity this press has produced billions of pieces of literature. Today, owing largely to Russell's foresight, the Watchtower Bible and Tract Society owns, among other things, whole blocks of valuable property in downtown Brooklyn, a large printing plant, a "Kingdom farm," and a missionary training school—Gilead—located in South Lansing, New York.

"Pastor" Russell continued his varied activities until his death in 1916 aboard a transcontinental train in Texas. His death brought to a close a most remarkable life, and one that will long be remembered in the annals of American cultism.

Charles Taze Russell might have been one of the great evangelists of the Christian Church had he subjugated his reasoning powers to the Holy Spirit, but instead he chose to crusade against the historical Church and its doctrine, and so died an unrewarded death.

Russell's career was also highly colored with moral and legal scandal, notably so in 1903, when Mrs. Russell (whom he married in 1880 and who had left him after seventeen years of marriage in 1897) sued the "Pastor" for divorce and was awarded a separation in 1906, following sensational testimony as to the "Pastor's" questionable habits with another woman, Rose Ball. In 1909 Russell was forced to pay his wife $6,036 in back alimony after it was shown that he deliberately transferred his property holdings to avoid payment.

Perhaps Russell is best known for promulgating the earliest of the Society's false prophecies concerning the end of the world. These false prophecies regarding Armageddon have characterized the Watchtower almost since its inception and have caused many Witnesses to become disillusioned with the "divine authority" controlling the Society. Over the years the Society has devised various methods for dealing with the charge of "false prophecy." They sometimes claim that they were only guessing at the future, but not claiming to speak prophecy in God's name. Sometimes they imply that the Society never promoted any particular dates: such notions were promulgated only by errant members. Sometimes they imply that new "light" supplies missing information which modifies their understanding of end-time chronology. Sometimes they use the easy way out—they reprint their earlier prophetic writings with the dates carefully changed, thereby erasing evidence of false prophesying.

The "Pastor," Charles Taze Russell, was a master at this. For example, in the early printings of his "commentary" series, *Studies in the Scriptures,* volume 2, entitled *The Time Is at Hand,* Russell very clearly predicted the end of the world in 1914. Quotes from page 77 of the 1910 edition read:

> ... 1914; and that that date will be the farthest
> limit of the rule of imperfect men .... at that
> date the Kingdom of God ... will obtain full,
> universal control, and that it will then be "set up,"
> or firmly established on the earth, on the ruins of
> present institutions .... it will prove that some
> time before the end of A.D. 1914 the last mem-
> ber of the divinely recognized Church of Christ
> ... will be glorified with the Head."[3]

However, the very *same* book, the very *same* page,
but published in *1914*, the supposed year of the end,
reads significantly differently at those same places:

> ... 1914; and that that date will *see the disinte-
> gration* of the rule of imperfect men .... at that
> date the Kingdom of God ... will *begin to
> assume* control, and that it will then *shortly* be
> "set up," or firmly established, in the earth, on
> the ruins of present institutions .... it will prove
> that some time before the end of *the overthrow*
> the last member of the divinely recognized
> Church of Christ ... will be glorified with the
> Head."[4]

There are a myriad of false prophecies concerning
the end of the world promulgated officially by the Watchtower Society over the years of its domination of misguided Jehovah's Witnesses.[5] Following is a listing of
some of those false prophecies. This listing shows the
depths of non-inspiration to which an organization can
sink when it claims to speak for Jehovah God and actually speaks only for misguided men who do not know
God's Word.

1899 " ... the 'battle of the great day of God Almighty' (Revelation 16:14), which will end in A.D. 1914 with the complete overthrow of earth's present rulership, is already commenced" (Charles Taze Russell, *The Time Is at Hand,* Brooklyn, NY: Watchtower Bible and Tract Society, 1908 ed., p. 101).

1897 "Our Lord, the appointed King, is now present, since October 1874" (Charles Taze Russell, *The Day of Vengeance,* 1897, p. 621).

1916 "The Bible chronology herein presented show that the six great 1000 year days beginning with Adam are ended, and that the great 7th Day, the 1000 years of Christ's Reign, began in 1873" (Charles Taze Russell, *The Time Is at Hand,* 1916 ed., p. ii).

1918 "Therefore we may confidently expect that 1925 will mark the return of Abraham, Isaac, Jacob, and the faithful prophets of old, particularly those named by the Apostle in Hebrews 11, to the condition of human perfection" (Joseph P. Rutherford, *Millions Now Living Will Never Die,* Brooklyn, NY: Watchtower Bible and Tract Society, 1918, p. 89).

1922 "The date 1925 is even more distinctly indicated by the Scriptures than 1914" (*Watchtower,* September 1, 1922, p. 262).

1923 "Our thought is, that 1925 is definitely settled by the Scriptures. As to Noah, the Christian now has much more upon which to base his faith than Noah had upon which to base his faith in a coming deluge" (*Watchtower,* April 1, 1923, p. 106).

1925 "The year 1925 is here. With great expectation Christians have looked forward to this year. Many have confidently expected that all members of the body of Christ will be changed to heavenly glory during this year. This may be accomplished. It may not be. In his own due time God will accomplish his purposes concerning his people. Christians should not be so deeply concerned about what may transpire this year" (*Watchtower*, January 1, 1925, p. 3).

September 1925 "It is to be expected that Satan will try to inject into the minds of the consecrated, the thought that 1925 should see an end to the work" (*Watchtower*, September 1, 1925, p. 262).

1926 "Some anticipated that the work would end in 1925, but the Lord did not state so" (*Watchtower*, August 1, 1926, p. 232).

1931 "There was a measure of disappointment on the part of Jehovah's faithful ones on earth concerning the years 1914, 1918, and 1925, which disappointment lasted for a time . . . and they also learned to quit fixing dates" (Joseph P. Rutherford, *Vindication*, book 1, pp. 338, 339).

1941 "Receiving the gift, the marching children clasped it to them, not a toy or plaything for idle pleasure, but the Lord's provided instrument for most effective work in the remaining months before Armageddon" (*Watchtower*, September 15, 1941, p. 288).

1968 "True, there have been those in times past who predicted an 'end to the world,' even announcing a specific date . . . . Yet nothing happened. The 'end' did not come. They were guilty of false prophesying. Why? What was missing? . . . Missing from such people were God's truths and the evidence that he was guiding and using them" (*Awake*, October 8, 1968, p. 23).

1968 "What about all this talk concerning the year 1975? . . . [Serious Bible students'] interest has been kindled by the belief that 1975 will mark the end of 6,000 years of human history since Adam's creation . . . . One thing is absolutely certain, Bible chronology reinforced with fulfilled Bible prophecy shows that six thousand years of man's existence will soon be up, yes, within this generation!" (*The Watchtower*, August 15, 1968, pp. 494,500).

1976 "It may be that some who have been serving God have planned their lives according to a mistaken view of just what was to happen on a certain date or in a certain year ... they have missed the point of the Bible's warnings concerning the end of this system of things, thinking the Bible chronology reveals the specific date .... But it is not advisable for us to set our sights on a certain date .... The chronology in the Bible is not there without good purpose. That chronology indicates that we are at the close of six thousand years of human history" (*Watchtower*, July 15, 1976, pp. 440-443).[6]

There are dozens more published incidents of false prophesying on the part of the Watchtower Society; these are merely representative. It should be abundantly clear from the above, however, that the Watchtower Society is guilty of false prophesying numerous times and that no one who desires to follow the commands of Scripture should follow the Watchtower. Instead we should heed the words of Deuteronomy 18:21-22: "And if thou say in thine heart, How shall we know the word which the Lord hath not spoken? When a prophet speaketh in the name of the Lord, if the thing follow not, nor come to pass, that is the thing which the Lord hath not spoken, but the prophet hath spoken it presumptuously: thou shalt not be afraid of him."

Instilling fear of an imminent apocalypse in those unlearned in the Scriptures may bring converts to one's cause, but it does not promote biblical truth. Both "Pastor" Russell and the Society officials after him will stand before the judgment of God for their parts in leading innocent people astray.

False prophesying was not the only fault to which "Pastor" Russell fell prey. His own scheme once backfired on him. He sued the Reverend J.J. Ross of Hamilton, Ontario, for libel over a pamphlet the latter had written, only to lose the case and prove himself a perjurer on the witness stand.[7]

Much, much more could be cited to show that Charles Taze Russell was not the caliber of man to trust in things of the Spirit, but despite this his writings had a circulation of twenty-five million copies, and the *Watchtower* of today still credits him as its founder and spreads many of his teachings. Jehovah's Witnesses of today, however, obtained their name from J.F. Rutherford, better known as the "Judge," in 1931. As Russell's trusted lawyer, Rutherford took over the movement in 1916 and ran it without question until his death from cancer in 1942. Nathan Homer Knorr took the reins of the Society at Rutherford's death, and it was under him that the Society began publishing all of its materials without credit to individual authors. Knorr retained some anonymity with the public, although all Witnesses looked to him as the final authority in the Society. Knorr died in June of 1977. Frederick W. Franz today pilots the *Watchtower,* and he continues in the same path as the "Pastor," the "Judge," and Knorr, all of whom have for the most part faded into the *Watchtower's* lengthening shadow.

THE THEOLOGY OF THE *WATCHTOWER*
The basic Christological tenet of Jehovah's Witnesses, or Russellism, is that utilized by the old Alexandrian theologian, Arius, in the third century, and which subsequently won for him the "distinction" of excommunication from the Christian Church as a result of the Council of Nicea in A.D. 325.

Like Arius, whom he emulated, Russell and the Jehovah's Witnesses rejected the doctrine of the Trinity categorically. In *Let God Be True,* p. 111, we read, "The trinity doctrine was not conceived by Jesus or the early Christians. Nowhere in the Scriptures is even any mention made of a trinity .... The plain truth is that this is another of Satan's attempts to keep God-fearing persons from learning the truth of Jehovah and his Son, Christ Jesus. No, there is no trinity!" In the place of the Trinity, the Witnesses accept Jesus as "a second god" or "a god," the first and greatest creation of Jehovah God.[8]

For Jehovah's Witnesses, the Lord Jesus was the archangel Michael prior to His arrival on earth, and while He was on earth He was only a perfect man who merited immortality by obedience to Jehovah's commands.[9]

Such a view is, of course, totally unscriptural, and has been thoroughly refuted in my book *Jehovah of the Watchtower,* along with all the other anti-biblical teachings of Jehovah's Witnesses.

For those who are interested in an exhaustive treatment of the subject, I recommend the lengthy chapter on Jehovah's Witnesses in my book *Kingdom of the Cults,* which covers many of the major American cult systems.

In concluding this outline of Jehovah's Witnesses, I have listed the following major doctrines of the movement, documented from the literature of the cult itself. These are verbatim quotations, not hearsay, and are therefor authentic and dependable.

The Trinity

This is what they think Christians believe concerning the Trinity: "The doctrine, in brief, is that there are three gods in one: 'God the Father, God the Son, and God the Holy Ghost,' all three equal in power, substance and eternity" (*Let God Be True,* p. 100, 1952 edition).[10]

1. "The obvious conclusion is, therefore, that Satan

is the originator of the trinity doctrine" (ibid., p. 101).

2. "The trinity doctrine was not conceived by Jesus or the early Christians" (ibid., p. 111).

The Deity of Jesus Christ

1. " . . . the true Scriptures speak of God's Son, the Word, as 'a god.' He is a 'mighty god,' but not the Almighty God, who is Jehovah" (*The Truth Shall Make You Free*, p. 47).

2. "In other words, he was the first and direct creation of Jehovah God" (*The Kingdom Is at Hand*, pp. 46-47, 49).

The Deity of the Holy Spirit

1. "As for the 'Holy Spirit,' the so-called 'third Person of the Trinity,' we have already seen that it is, not a person, but God's active force" (*The Truth That Leads to Eternal Life*, 1968 ed., p. 24).

2. "The Scriptures themselves unite to show that God's holy spirit is not a person but is God's *active force* by which he accomplishes his purpose and executes his will" (*Aid to Bible Understanding*, 1971 ed., p. 1543).

The Atonement of Christ

1. "That which is redeemed or brought back is what was lost, namely, perfect human life, with its rights and earthly prospects" (*Let God Be True*, p. 114).

The Resurrection of Christ

1. "The firstborn [Christ] from the dead was raised from the grave, not a human creature, but a spirit" (ibid., p. 276).

2. "So the King Christ Jesus was put to death in the flesh and was resurrected an invisible spirit creature" (ibid., p. 138).

The Return of Christ

They claim it has already occurred invisibly in 1914-1918.

1. "It does not mean that he [Christ] is on the way or has promised to come, but that he has already arrived and is here" (ibid., p. 198).

2. "Jesus Christ returns, not again as a human, but as a glorious spirit person" (ibid., p. 196).

Human Government

1. " . . . hence no witness of Jehovah, who ascribes salvation only to Him, may salute any national emblem without violating Jehovah's commandment against idolatry as stated in his Word" (ibid., p. 243).

The Existence of Hell and Eternal Punishment

1. "It is so plain that the Bible hell is mankind's common grave that even an honest little child can understand it, but not the religious theologians" (ibid., p. 92).

2. " . . . those who have been taught by Christendom to believe the God-dishonoring doctrine of a fiery hell for tormenting conscious human souls eternally" (ibid., p. 88).

3. "The doctrine of a burning hell where the wicked are tortured eternally after death cannot be true, mainly for four reasons: (1) It is wholly unscriptural; (2) It is unreasonable; (3) It is contrary to God's love; and (4) It is repugnant to justice" (*ibid.,* p. 99).

4. " . . . The promulgator of it is Satan himself . . . " (ibid., p. 98).

Satan—The Devil

1. "The ultimate end of Satan is complete annihilation" (ibid., p. 64).

The Existence of the Soul

1. " . . . man is a combination of two things, namely, the 'dust of the ground' and 'the breath of life.' The combining of these two things (or factors) produced a living soul or creature called *man*" (ibid., p. 68).

2. "So we see that the claim of religionists that man has an immortal soul and therefore differs from the beast is not Scriptural" (ibid., p. 68).

3. "Thus it is seen that the serpent (the Devil) is the one that originated the doctrine of the inherent immortality of human souls" (ibid., pp. 74-75).

The Kingdom of Heaven

1. "The undefeatable purpose of Jehovah God to establish a righteous kingdom in these last days was fulfilled A.D. 1914" (ibid., p. 143).

2. "Who and how many are able to enter it [the Kingdom]? The Revelation limits to 144,000 the number that become a part of the Kingdom and stand on heavenly Mount Zion—Revelation 14:1,3; 7:4-8" (ibid., p. 136).

In the light of these obvious denials of Scripture and Christianity, the interested Christian and non-Christian alike might well take warning about this counterfeit of Christ's gospel. Jehovah's Witnesses or the Watchtower Bible and Tract Society is no more than another name for Russellism, the teachings of Charles Taze Russell, a false scholar and religious imposter who made merchandise of the Christian faith. Jehovah's Witnesses, of course, maintain that they do not follow "Pastor" Russell, but this is a deliberate falsehood, as has been shown by their doctrines and their references to him and his writings.

The end product of this cult is a subtle denial of our Lord Jesus Christ—His true deity, resurrection, and return. The Witnesses have never ceased to dishonor

Him regarding these points of revelation, making a mere creature of God's eternal Son who died for all men to purchase for us a home in heaven, not a Russellite paradise on earth.

A CHRISTIAN RESPONSE

Although space precludes a thorough and complete refutation of all heretical points of Watchtower theology, the following is a brief biblical response to the specific heresies chronicled above.

The Trinity

We do not believe in three gods in one. All biblical Christians believe that within the nature of the one true God (Isa. 43:10; 1 Cor. 8:4-6) there are three eternally distinct Persons (Luke 1:35): the Father (2 Pet. 1:17); the Word or Son (John 1:1,14); and the Holy Spirit (Acts 5:3-4). These three Persons are (is) the One God (Matt. 28:19). The doctrine of the Holy Trinity has been part of the historic Christian Church's confession since apostolic times. It is essential to biblical teaching.

The Deity of Jesus Christ

The doctrine of the absolute deity of Jesus Christ has also always been part of the historic Christian Church's confession. He is not "a god" (such a belief would be polytheism, or belief in more than one god) and is not created. He is the Eternal God, Second Person of the Holy Trinity, manifested in the flesh (John 1:1,14). There was never a time when the Second Person did not exist. There are numerous verses in the Bible attesting to the absolute deity of Jesus Christ, to His essential and necessary equality with the Father and the Spirit. Some of these verses include Luke 1:41-43; John 1:1,14; John 5:18; John 8:58-59; John 10:30; John 20:28; Romans 1:3-4; 9:5; Philippians 2:5-11; Colossians 1:15-16; Colossians 2:9; Titus 2:13; Hebrews 1:6-8; 1 John 5:20; and Revelation 22:13.

The Deity of the Holy Spirit

As intrinsic as is the deity of Jesus Christ to the doctrine of the Trinity is the deity (and necessary personality) of the Holy Spirit. It has always been the teaching of the church, taken from the Scriptures, that the Holy Spirit is a person distinct from the Father and the Son as far as His person is concerned and yet one with the Father and Son as far as His nature is concerned. The Holy Spirit is absolute God. Attributes which can only be ascribed to a person are ascribed in the Scriptures to the Holy Spirit. Actions only performable by a person are ascribed in the Scriptures to the Holy Spirit. Finally, the Holy Spirit is several times affirmed to be God by nature. Verses relating to the personality and deity of the Holy Spirit include Psalm 104:30; John 3:5; John 14:26; John 15:26; John 16:7-15; Acts 5:3-4; Acts 10:19-20; Acts 13:2; Acts 28:25-27; Romans 8:26; 1 Corinthians 2:10; 1 Corinthians 12:11; and Hebrews 9:14.

The Atonement of Christ

The sacrifice of the Lord Jesus Christ on the cross for our sins was much more than the sacrifice of a perfect man (Jesus) for a fallen man (Adam). As the writer of Luke records, the church of God was purchased with God's "own blood" (Acts 20:28). As the God-man, fully divine and fully human, Jesus Christ's sacrifice was whole and complete. He was the representative of the fallen world (man), operating as priest (holy), the sacrifice Himself (lamb), and the one to whom all must be reconciled (God). Verses relating to the biblical doctrine of the atonement include Leviticus 17:11; John 1:29; 2 Corinthians 5:20; Colossians 1:20; Hebrews 9:22; and 1 Peter 2:24.

The Resurrection of Christ

Jesus Christ was not raised "a spirit creature." On the contrary, the Scriptures are adamant in asserting that His resurrection was the resurrection of the same body which had hung on the cross but which had been glorified and transformed. In fact, the bodily resurrection of Jesus Christ is a guarantee and a representation of what the resurrection of believers will be like.

In John 2:19-21 Jesus Christ prophesied the nature of His resurrection when He declared, "Destroy this temple, and in three days I will raise it up." The disciples understood and remembered when He rose from the dead that "he spake of the temple of his body" (v. 21). Immediately after the Resurrection the disciples themselves were confused and at one appearance of the risen Christ were afraid, "and supposed that they had seen a spirit" (Luke 24:37). This is just the mistake Jehovah's Witnesses make! However, Jesus set them straight by replying, "Why are ye troubled? and why do thoughts arise in your hearts? Behold my hands and my feet, that it is I myself: handle me, and see; for *a spirit hath not flesh and bones, as ye see me have*" (vv. 38-39, italics added). Other verses which describe the bodily resurrection include John 20:27-28; Mark 16:14; and 1 Corinthians 15:15.

The Return of Christ

The Scriptures are unanimous in affirming the visible and physical return of Jesus Christ, the doctrine known in church history as the Second Coming. In fact, Revelation 1:7 asserts that every eye will behold him, "even those that pierced him." Other verses on the Second Coming include Matthew 24:30; 1 Thessalonians 4:16-17; and Zechariah 12:10.

Human Government

While the Bible does not delineate exactly the proper role of government in the believer's life and the responsibility of the believer to his earthly government, it clearly does not describe the narrow and almost paranoid rejection of almost all government promoted by the Watchtower Society. A careful study of Romans 13:1-7 would be a good foundation for understanding the basic relationship of believer to earthly government.

The Existence of Hell and Eternal Punishment (and the Destiny of Satan—the Devil)

One of the clearest verses of Scripture affirming the existence of hell as a place of eternal and conscious punishment is found in Matthew 25:46. As eternal and conscious as eternal life will be, that is how eternal and conscious eternal punishment will be: "And these shall go away into everlasting punishment: but the righteous into life eternal." Other verses concerning the nature of hell include Matthew 5:22; 8:11-12; 13:42,50; 2 Peter 2:17; and Jude 13.

The Existence of the Soul

While the term *immortality* more properly refers to the ongoing endless existence of the resurrected believers' bodies, it is the teaching of Scripture, contrary to the Watchtower belief, that the immaterial part of man also exists consciously and endlessly. We have seen above that the unrighteous will exist in an eternal state of conscious punishment. It is also biblical to believe that the righteous will exist in an eternal state of conscious fellowship with God. That the soul is not part of the material part of man is evident from many Scriptures, some of which include Genesis 1:26; 5:1; Job 32:8; Acts 7:59; 1 Corinthians 2:11; and 2 Corinthians 5:1-9.

The Kingdom of Heaven

It is reprehensible that the Watchtower Society teaches that heaven is an elitist "club" to which only 144,000 "faithful" can ever belong. On the contrary, the Bible clearly teaches that anyone who loves God is born of God (1 John 4:7), and that anyone who is born of God can and will enter the kingdom of heaven (John 3:5). Luke 17:20-26 and Revelation 7:9; 22:1-14 tell us more about the kingdom of heaven and its inhabitants.

From this chapter it is clear that the Jehovah's Witnesses, the followers of apostate Charles Taze Russell and of the heretical teachings of the Watchtower Bible and Tract Society, are in a cult. Jehovah's Witnesses do not represent the God of the Bible. They, knowingly or not, represent a manufactured god who is unable to save anyone. With compassion, patience, and understanding we must reach out to those lost in the Watchtower and extend to them the true gospel, the biblical faith, concerning Jesus Christ, "our great God and Savior" (Titus 2:13).

NOTES

1. Brooklyn, N.Y.: Watchtower Bible and Tract Society, 1961, p. 1151.

2. For more information, see Michael Van Buskirk's *The Scholastic Dishonesty of the Watchtower* (P.O. Box 2067, Costa Mesa, CA: Christian Apologetics: Research and Information Service, 1976).

3. Charles Taze Russell, *Studies in the Scriptures,* vol. 2, *The Time Is at Hand* (Brooklyn, NY: Watchtower Bible and Tract Society, 1910), p. 77.

4. Ibid.

5. A cult-watching organization known for its excellent evangelistic efforts to Jehovah's Witnesses has complete documentation from original sources concerning Jehovah's Witnesses' many false prophecies. Inquiries (including a self-addressed, stamped envelope) should be directed to Christian Apologetics: Research and Information Service, P.O. Box 2067, Costa Mesa, CA 92626.

6. This information is available in tract form, "One Hundred Years of Divine Direction?" from my Christian Research Institute, P.O. Box 500, San Juan Capistrano, CA 92693.

7. For a thorough discussion of the entire Jehovah's Witnesses movement, see Walter Martin, *Jehovah of the Watchtower,* 8th ed., rev. and enl., (Minneapolis: Bethany House Publishers, 1975).

8. See John 1:1 in *The New World Translation of the Holy Scriptures.*

9. See *Awake,* June 22, 1955, p. 9.

10. Unless otherwise stated, this second edition is meant.

three
The Maze of Mormonism

The Church of Jesus Christ of Latter-day Saints, commonly known as the Mormons, traces its heritage all the way back to a supernatural angelic vision given to its founder, Joseph Smith, Jr., in the early 1800s.[1] How can we test the message of this or any other "angelic messenger"? The Holy Bible, God's original and perfect revelation to mankind (Heb. 1:1), gives a test in Galatians 1:6-9:

"I marvel that ye are so soon removed from him that called you into the grace of Christ unto another gospel: which is not another; but there be some that trouble you, and would pervert the gospel of Christ. But though we, *or an angel from heaven,* preach any other gospel unto you than that which we have preached unto you, let him be accursed. As we said before, so say I now again, if any man preach any other gospel unto you than that ye have received, let him be accursed" (italics added).

From this passage we know that any "angelic" message *must* be in harmony with what God has already revealed in His Word, the Bible, and in the person of the Incarnate Word, Jesus Christ our Lord. First Thessalonians 5:21-22 admonishes us, saying, "Prove all things; hold fast that which is good. Abstain from all appearance of evil." Even 1 John 4:1 warns, "Beloved, believe not every spirit, but try the spirits whether they are of God: because many false prophets are gone out into the world." So, we have ample instruction from Scripture on testing messages which claim to come from God and a serious responsibility as believers to submit to the judgment of God's Word on such matters. As we shall see in our present study, Mormon doctrine cannot pass the test of biblical scrutiny. We shall see that Mormonism teaches polytheism, or the belief in more than one God, a teaching openly refuted in the Bible. Mormonism teaches a five-fold path to salvation, denying the biblical doctrine of justification by faith alone. Mormonism denies the biblical deity of Christ and the virgin birth. Mormonism denies the authority of the Bible.

We are not "attacking" good Mormon people: we are holding the Mormon "gospel" to the light of the Bible and finding it black and corrupt. Such an examination is encouraged in word if not in deed by the Mormon church itself. Brigham Young, successor to "Prophet" Smith declared, "Take up the Bible, compare the religion of the Latter-Day Saints with it, and see if it will stand the test."[2] Mormon apostle Orson Pratt even urged, " . . . convince us of our errors of doctrine, if we have any, by reason, by logical arguments, or by the word of God, and we will be ever grateful for the information, and you will ever have the pleasing reflection that you have been instruments in the hands of God of redeeming your fellow beings from the darkness which you may see enveloping their minds."[3]

With the Bible as our guide we will examine the claims of Mormonism, discovering that those claims are spurious and empty. The prophets of Mormonism would teach us to believe in many gods, and even that we can, through a process, become gods ourselves! This absolutely contradicts the test of a prophet from God given in Deuteronomy 13:1-4: "If there arise among you a prophet, or a dreamer of dreams, and giveth thee a sign or a wonder, and the sign or the wonder come to pass, whereof he spake unto thee, saying, Let us go after other gods, which thou hast not known, and let us serve them; thou shalt not hearken unto the words of that prophet, or that dreamer of dreams: for the Lord your God proveth you, to know whether ye love the Lord your God with all your heart and with all your soul. Ye shall walk after the Lord your God, and fear him, and keep his commandments, and obey his voice, and ye shall serve him, and cleave unto him."

We can know that any who claim to be prophets of God must identify God correctly. Any who would have us worship a God other than the one true and almighty God of the Bible are false prophets, an offense serious enough that those false prophets under the Old Testament theocracy were put to death for their blasphemy. What is Mormonism? What does it teach? Where did it come from? How can we share the gospel with sincere but deceived Mormons? These questions we shall answer below.

Of all the major cults extant in the melting pot of religions called American, none is more subtle or dangerous to the unwary soul than the Church of Jesus Christ of Latter-day Saints, the official name for Mormonism. This stalwart organization is composed of over 5.1 million members, all active in zealously promoting the "revelations" of "Prophet" Joseph Smith and the indomitable Brigham Young. Ruled by a first president and a supreme council ironically titled the "Twelve Apostles," the Mormon religion stretches the length and breadth of our country and reaches even to numerous foreign mission fields throughout the world. Indeed, with its tremendous wealth, growing prestige, and zeal for missionary programs, Mormonism constitutes an immense threat to the Church of Jesus Christ of our era.

From Salt Lake City, Utah, the hub of the Mormon wheel of ever-expanding influence, over sixty thousand energetic Mormon missionaries travel each year two-by-two, even as the apostles of old, in order to carry one of the cleverest counterfeits of the true gospel yet devised, one which stands ready to ensnare the souls of a world rich in religion and bankrupt in the faith that saves. Today Mormonism is powerful, its missionary program immense, and its inroads upon the Christian faith tragic. But what type of doctrine is it that appeals so much to the modern mind that orthodox Christianity suffers as a result? Who brought about this Mormon religion which today plagues our mission fields? What do Mormons believe, and how can they be evangelized effectively and their influence combatted? These questions are being asked by concerned Christian pastors, evangelists, and laymen everywhere as they recognize the threat of Mormonism and the need for a definite plan of action to meet the growing challenge at home and abroad. Let us therefore examine the history and doctrines of this "new gospel," which found its origin not in the inspired writings of the New Testament but in the mind of one Joseph Smith, Jr., in the year 1830.

THE MORMON PROPHET

Joseph Smith, Jr., founder of the Mormon religion, was born in Sharon, Vermont, on December 23, 1805. He was the son of a poverty-stricken, part-time treasure hunter who spent his time dabbling in the occult and searching for Captain Kidd's treasure.[4] Young "Joe," as he was irreverently referred to in his pre-prophet days, early gained the reputation of being the biggest faker of the entire Smith family, and was engaged for the most part of his youth in seeking Captain Kidd's treasure and in gazing through "peep stones" in which, he declared to superstitious neighbors, he could see their futures. This charge, long debated, was validated by an articulate historian, Rev. Wesley P. Walters. While in Norwich, New York, Rev. Walters searched through the Chenango County's "dead storage" and, on July 28, 1971, uncovered the justice's and constable's bills of a March 20, 1826 trial in which Joseph Smith, Jr., was labeled "the glass looker," and was convicted for this misdemeanor, resulting in a small fine. A personal account from Pomeroy Tucker, a man who was personally acquainted with the Smith family, can best portray the early character of Joseph Smith. Witness his unprejudiced testimony:

At this period in the life and career of Joseph Smith, Jr., or 'Joe Smith,' as he was universally named, and the Smith family, they were popularly regarded as an illiterate, whiskey-drinking, shiftless, irreligious race of people—the first named, the chief subject of this biography, being unanimously voted the laziest and most worthless of the generation. From the age of twelve to twenty years he is distinctly remembered as a dull-eyed, flaxen-haired, prevaricating boy—noted only for his indolent and vagabondish character, and his habits of exaggeration and untruthfulness. Taciturnity was among his characteristic idiosyncrasies, and he seldom spoke to anyone outside of his intimate associates, except when first addressed by another; and then, by reason of the extravagances of his statement, his word was received with the least confidence by those who knew him best. He could utter the most palpable exaggeration or marvelous absurdity with the utmost apparent gravity.[5]

Further than this, the following testimony was given by prominent members of the community in which the Smith family lived:

We, the undersigned, have been acquainted with the Smith family, for a number of years, while they resided near this place, and we have no hesitation in saying, that we consider them destitute of that moral character, which ought to entitle them to the confidence of any community. They were particularly famous for visionary projects, spent much of their time in digging for money which they pretended was hid in the earth, and to this day, large excavations may be seen in the earth, not far from their residence, where they used to spend their time in digging for hidden treasures. Joseph Smith, Senior, and his son Joseph were, in particular, considered entirely destitute of *moral character, and addicted to vicious habits.*

We, the undersigned, being personally acquainted with the family of Joseph Smith, Sen., with whom the celebrated Gold Bible, so-called, originated, state: that they were not only a lazy, indolent set of men, but also intemperate; and their word was not to be depended upon; and that we are truly glad to dispense with their society.[6]

This is a far different picture from that so vividly manufactured by numerous Mormon historians. It should be noted that this is contemporary evidence, not the product of flowery Mormon historians who have distorted the true character of Smith and portrayed him as a noble, self-sacrificing youth dedicated to the gospel of Christ and the Bible, which history tells us he emphatically was not!

One thing which Mormon missionaries are careful to avoid when visiting prospective converts is a truthful accounting of what is known as Joseph Smith's First Vision. This vision was supposed to have occurred in 1820, in the midst of a revival (that secular history tells us actually could not have occurred until 1824). According to the record in the *Pearl of Great Price* Smith said:

> ... immediately I was seized upon by some power which entirely overcame me, and had such an astonishing influence over me as to bind my tongue so that I could not speak. Thick darkness gathered around me, and it seemed to me for a time as if I were doomed to sudden destruction.
>
> But, exerting all my powers to call upon God to deliver me out of the power of this enemy which had seized upon me, and at the very moment when I was ready to sink into despair and abandon myself to destruction—not to an imaginary ruin, but to the power of some actual being from the unseen world, who had such

marvelous power as I had never before felt in any being—just at this moment of great alarm, I saw a pillar of light exactly over my head, above the brightness of the sun, which descended gradually until it fell upon me.

It no sooner appeared than I found myself delivered from the enemy which held me bound.[7]

Smith was told immediately that *all* religions/sects were wrong, that "all of their creeds were an abomination in his sight," and that all of their members were corrupt.[8]

The First Vision of Joseph Smith Jr. is of paramount importance to the Mormon church. It is the centerpiece in almost all Mormon presentations of Smith's prophetic authority. The First Vision forms the basis for the Mormon doctrine that God the Father and Jesus Christ *both* have flesh and bone bodies and are in fact two separate gods. This vision also teaches that the Christian Church was in apostasy before Smith founded the Mormon church and that God designated Smith to be the prophet of the restoration of true Christianity. The core of the vision contains the following account:

My object in going to inquire of the Lord was to know which of all the sects was right, that I might know which to join. No sooner, therefore, did I get possession of myself, so as to be able to speak, than I asked the Personages who stood above me in the light, which of all the sects was right—and which I should join.

I was answered that I must join none of them, for they were all wrong; and the Personage who addressed me said that all their creeds were an abomination in his sight; that those professors were all corrupt; that "they draw near to me with their lips, but their hearts are far from me, they teach for doctrines the commandments of men, having a form of godliness, but they deny the power thereof."[9]

When we examine the historical evidence, however, we find that the record of this "First Vision" is strangely muddled and contradictory. In *Journal of Discourses* 13:77-78, we are informed that *an angel* appeared to Smith. The revised edition of the story says that it was *God the Father and Jesus Christ.* In 1833 Joseph Smith gave an account of his First Vision in which he omitted any mention of having seen God the Father as well as the condemnation of all Christian churches and people.[10]

Based on this confused vision and its successors and the word of a convicted fortune-teller, the Mormon church was founded on April 6, 1830 with Joseph Smith installed as "Prophet, Seer, and Revelator." The church was founded in New York, shortly moved to Pennsylvania and then Ohio, spent time in Missouri and Illinois, and eventually became the nucleus for a new town, Nauvoo, in Illinois. In Nauvoo, Joseph's word was the last word, and he appropriated for himself the titles of "General" and "Chief Justice" of the municipal court of Nauvoo. By this time Smith was teaching polygamy openly and church/community membership was around two thousand.

However, persecution also followed the cult and often Smith and other members suffered for their deviant behavior. In the spring of 1844, Smith and his brother Hyrum were jailed in nearby Carthage, Illinois on suspicion of destroying the printing press of a critical and rival newspaper. On June 27, 1844 a mob stormed the jail and in the ensuing gun battle (Smith and Hyrum had had guns smuggled to them in jail), the Smith brothers were killed. The Mormons refer to this as Joseph's martyrdom, but since they shot and wounded several of their attackers they do not really qualify as ones who die willingly for their faith.

Upon the death of Joseph Smith, Brigham Young, devoted disciple of the "Prophet," grasped the helm of the faltering Mormon bark and steered a straight course westward, bound on finding a place where the followers of the "new revelation" might settle peacefully, unhampered by the great mass of mankind who believed that one wife is enough for any home and that the gospel of Jesus Christ was sufficiently plain without "Prophet" Smith's "revelations" to "explain" it. The Mormons finally settled near what is now Salt Lake City, Utah, and founded a small, extremely powerful kingdom ruled by Young and the "Twelve Apostles," whose word was life and death to those who chose the Mormon religion. In this little kingdom polygamy flourished openly, and it was only near the turn of the century that this unchristian practice was outlawed. Despite the enforcement of the law, however, there are still some sects of Mormon origin, misnamed "Fundamentalists," who practice polygamy today.

Today the Mormons enjoy good public support and many Mormons are prominent business and social figures. Several top actors and actresses are open and dedicated Mormons. The vast Marriott hotel chain family is staunchly Mormon. Mormon politicians are influential in many state and federal government positions. The Mormons have come a long way from the early days of persecution and ridicule when Smith was considered little more than a vagabond and con man.[11]

The four inspired scriptures of the Mormons include the Bible ("insofar as it is translated correctly"), the *Book of Mormon,* the *Pearl of Great Price,* and *Doctrine and Covenants.* The Mormon inclusion of the Bible as inspired Scripture is more gratuitous than actual. Since so many Mormon doctrines are flatly contradicted by the Bible, the only recourse for the hapless Mormon is to assume (contrary to the evidence) that the Bible "must have been mistranslated" and that "precious portions have been lost." In practice this translates to "the Bible is alright until it contradicts Mormon doctrine. Then it can't be trusted."

The *Book of Mormon* contains what purports to be the record of the Jews and Jesus Christ in North and South America. As mentioned above, it is not actually a sacred revelation of God. It is a purloined novel in disguise!

The *Pearl of Great Price* contains part of the history of the church and of Joseph Smith and the controversial "Book of Abraham," the Mormon justification for racial discrimination based on the words of the biblical patriarch Abraham.

Doctrine and Covenants contains many of the revelations given by God to Smith and some given to his successor, Brigham Young. This volume clearly teaches polygamy and the plurality of gods.

THE MORMON REVELATION

The general story of how Smith received his "revelation" is a most genuine piece of fantasy and would be occasion for genuine laughter were it not for the tragic fact that over five million people believe it as divine truth.

As the story goes, young Smith, bent on serving the true God, was the recipient of a vision in which both the Father and the Son spoke to him, despaired of the failure of Christendom to dispense the gospel, and anointed the humble Joseph "Prophet of the Restored Christian

Religion."[12] Accompanying these celestial manifestations, a most obliging angel, Moroni by name, inter-
viewed young Smith in the course of time. Moroni
entrusted to the fledgling prophet the privilege of trans-
lating the "Golden Plates" of what later became the fabu-
lous *Book of Mormon,* which was among other things a
dismal plagiarism of the King James Bible.[13] The
thoughtful angel also provided the illiterate Smith with a
pair of miraculous spectacles, Urim and Thummim with
the aid of which Joe "translated" the Golden Plates for
posterity. Smith's cohort in the preparation of this gigantic hoax was one Martin Harris, by turn a Quaker, Univer-
salist, Baptist, Presbyterian, and religious adventurer
whose sanity, it was said by contemporaries, would have
been hard to establish in a court of law.

Various Mormon historians have striven vainly to
establish the veracity of the *Book of Mormon,* which,
along with the *Pearl of Great Price* and *Doctrine and
Covenants,* makes up the central written authority of the
Mormon faith.[14] But the weight of evidence is far too
great for history to allow this sham to be cloaked in the
finery of saintly language and masqueraded as divine
revelation. The *Book of Mormon* contains literally hun-
dreds of readings lifted almost bodily from the King
James Bible, and it repeatedly reveals the linguistic
shortcomings of the "Prophet" Smith. It should be
noted, incidentally, that the *Book of Mormon* supposedly antedates the King James Bible by many, many
centuries; yet in numerous places the readings from it
are identical with the English version.

The second sacred book of the Mormon religion is
Doctrine and Covenants. It is a collection of revelations
given by God to Joseph Smith. The first "revelations"
were taken down from Smith's speeches by his scribes,
compiled, and published as the *Book of Command-*

ments. In 1835 the "revelations" were "corrected" and printed again, with subsequent revelations, as *Doctrine and Covenants.* There are at least sixty-five thousand changes between the first *Book of Commandments* and today's *Doctrine and Covenants.*

The third sacred book of the Mormons is the *Pearl of Great Price,* a compilation of different writings including supposedly ancient Hebrew Scriptures (the *Book of Abraham,* which discriminates against blacks), roughly revised biblical material, latter day revelations (called the *Articles of Faith*), and a life of Joseph Smith titled the *History of Joseph Smith the Prophet.* The *Articles of Faith* maintains, among other things, that the Bible can be trusted only insofar as it is "translated correctly," while the *Book of Mormon* is the Word of God without reservation.

These three books, with the Bible, comprise the four Mormon "scriptures." With the exception of the Bible, the Mormon scriptures are contradictory, unreliable historically and factually, and totally without divine inspiration. The Bible warns those who desire to speak with divine authority, saying, "Every word of God is pure: he is a shield unto them that put their trust in him. Add thou not unto his words, lest he reprove thee, and thou be found a liar" (Prov. 30:5-6).

STATEMENT OF FAITH

The statement of faith published by the Mormon church reads in many places like a declaration of orthodox theology; however, it is in reality a clever and, I believe, deliberate attempt to deceive the naive into believing that Mormonism is a Christian religion, which it is not in any sense of the term. All Mormons recognize Joseph Smith as a prophet and his words as binding, and thus the words of Smith carry as much if not more authority than the revealed Word of God. Mormonism differs from evangelical Christianity in five major ways and in numerous minor points which time does not allow us to discuss here.

THE TRINITY

Mormons deny the scriptural doctrine of the Trinity and the deity of the Lord Jesus Christ. To the Mormon mind God is a corporeal being even as we are, literally flesh and bones, and, said "Prophet" Brigham Young, "Adam is our father and our God and the only God with whom we have to do."[15] Historically, Mormon theology teaches that Adam-God entered Eden with Eve, one of His celestial wives, and the result of this physical union produced the human race.

Further than this, Joseph Smith himself wrote: "The Father has a body of flesh and bones . . . the Son also; but the Holy Ghost has not a body of flesh and bones but is a personage of Spirit. Were it not so, the Holy Ghost could not dwell in us."[16] It may be seen from this that the Mormon concept of God is completely foreign to that given in the Bible, for as Christ Himself said, "God is spirit, and those who worship him must worship in spirit and truth" (John 4:24, *RSV*). Mormonism seeks to reduce God to a carnal plane and even ascribes to him human methods of reproduction fully in keeping with the immoral and polygamous characters of Smith and Young, who allegedly had twenty-seven wives each, and the latter fifty-six children.

THE SCRIPTURES

Mormonism denies the authority of the Bible and, as has been shown, flatly contradicts the very Saviour in whom they profess to believe. The Bible clearly teaches that it, as interpreted by the Holy Spirit, is the sole authority for faith and morals, but Mormons equate the *Book of Mormon* with the Bible despite the fact that it has been shown to be a gigantic fraud and very possibly a deliberate plagiarism on the part of Smith and his cohort.

JESUS CHRIST

Historic Mormon theology denies the virgin birth of our Lord Jesus Christ and maintains instead that He was not conceived by the Holy Spirit but by Adam-God, who descended to earth and generated Jesus in the womb of Mary by sexual union. This shocking and vile concept is found in the writings of Brigham Young, who shamelessly wrote: "When the virgin Mary conceived the child Jesus the Father had begotten Him in His own likeness. He was not begotten by the Holy Ghost. And who was the Father? He was the first of the human family [Adam]."[17] One could search all the pages of Greek mythology and never surpass this display of sensual wickedness, and yet over 5.1 million people apply such blasphemy to the Son of God, who, Scripture tells us, was generated by the Holy Spirit and born of the virgin Mary without the aid of human agency (Luke 1:3-35).

SALVATION

The Mormon church denies emphatically the great and true biblical doctrine of justification before God on the basis of faith alone. The Apostle Paul tells us, "Therefore being justified by faith, we have peace with God through our Lord Jesus Christ" (Rom. 5:1). Indeed, the foundation stone of our hope is that God has nothing against us, and has forgiven our sins because Christ has died in our place. But a far different view is espoused by the Mormon church, as witnessed by their teaching: "The sectarian dogma of justification by faith alone has exercised an influence for evil."[18] It is a fairly simple matter to see from this bold declaration that Mormonism is not compatible with the Bible; indeed, it is apparent that the Bible is only a convenient tool by which they attract attention to their subtle and ever-misleading dogmas of deception.

THE ATONEMENT

The Mormon doctrine of the atonement of Christ is a far different one from that revealed in the Bible. The Scriptures irrevocably teach that Christ, the "Lamb of God," (John 1:29) "bare our sins in his own body on the tree" (1 Pet. 2:24), and that His blood alone is efficacious for the penalty of human sin. We are constantly reminded in the Bible that Christ died to purchase for us eternal life; not a sensual earthly paradise thriving on polygamy and the indulgence of human lusts, but a home "eternal in the heavens," one that "fadeth not away."

This is a far cry from Mormon mythology, which, like Russellism, teaches that all the atonement purchased for man was a "resurrection," an earthly paradise with the prospect of everlasting fertility and connubial bliss in the tradition of King Solomon's harem! In the words of the late president of the Mormon church, John Taylor, " . . . what was lost in Adam was restored in Christ . . . . Transgressions of the law brought death upon all the posterity of Adam, the restoration through the atonement restored all the human family to life . . . . The atonement made by Jesus Christ resulted in the resurrection of the human body."[19]

There are many other fundamental differences between the theology of Christianity and the theology of Mormonism. For more extensive information I refer the reader to two of my other books *The Maze of Mormon-*

ism and *The Kingdom of the Cults.*

The menace of Mormonism is the fact that it cleverly coats large doses of error with a thin layer of sugary half-truths and seemingly plausible reasons. By setting up a scale of punishment and sensuous rewards after death, Mormonism appeals to many persons who do not feel they are bad enough to go to hell or good enough to go straight to heaven, but who like the idea of a place where suffering does not exist but exile and a chance for future glory does. This proves most attractive to numerous individuals who do not have a sound grounding in biblical theology.

To board the Mormon train one needs a strong imagination, a supreme ego, and a firm conviction that no church on earth is true except the one founded by the "Prophet" Joseph Smith. The ego is needed because Mormon males believe they are potentially gods (in a higher or lower sense depending upon their faithfulness to the "Prophet" and his teachings) and that their destiny is sealed. They believe that someday they shall rule a polygamous universe presided over by their flesh-and-bone god, innumerable celestial wives, and "Prophet" Smith.[20]

In the light of these startling facts and the alarming spread and popularity of the Mormon religion, devout Christians must now take a definite stand; we can hesitate no longer. Four steps are needed immediately, I believe, to check the Mormon menace. They are as follows:

1. A program of education aimed at aiding pastors, teachers, and laymen to recognize the threat of Mormonism and the need for strong countermeasures.

2. The circulation of up-to-date and factual literature on the history, doctrines, and methods of Mormon progress, especially in the Midwest, on the Pacific Coast,

and in Hawaii and Africa.

3. A continual supply to worldwide mission fields of information on Mormon missionary activities, so that Mormonism may be kept under constant surveillance both at home and abroad.

4. A steady flow of consecrated Christian doctrine through churches, Bible schools, colleges, and seminaries dedicated to training our future leaders in a sound apologetic background so vital to combatting all forms of false doctrine which appear so prevalent in these, the last days of the age of grace.

It is the fundamental thesis of this writer that until Christians everywhere realize the danger of the cultism so clearly portrayed in the rise of the Mormon cult, evangelical efforts will continue to suffer on all mission fields, foreign and domestic, from those people of whom our Lord warned us, "Beware of false prophets, which come to you in sheep's clothing, but inwardly they are ravening wolves" (Matt. 7:15).

Let us awake to the dangers before us: the cultist wolf is at the door of the sheepfold. "He that hath ears to hear, let him hear."

NOTES

1. In actuality, Joseph Smith, Jr., most probably developed Mormonism from using a stolen and plagiarized novel written by Solomon Spalding and stolen from him by Sidney Rigdon, who later became a leading Mormon. It is Spalding's unpublished novel *Manuscript Found* which is almost certainly the basis for the *Book of Mormon*. For further information on this topic, see my book *The Maze of Mormonism* (Ventura, CA: Vision House, 1978) and *Who Really Wrote the Book of Mormon?* by Cowdrey, Davis and Scales (Ventura, CA: Vision House, 1977).

2. Brigham Young, *Journal of Discourses,* 16:46.

3. Orson Pratt, *The Seer, pp. 15-16.*

4. Wm. Alexander Linn, *The Story of the Mormons* (New York: Macmillan Co., 1902), p. 10.

5. Pomeroy Tucker, *The Origin, Rise and Progress of Mormonism* (New York: D. Appleton and Co., 1867), p. 16.

6. E.D. Howe, *Mormonism Unvailed* (Painesville, OH: Self-published, 1834), pp. 261-262.

7. Joseph Smith, Jr., *Pearl of Great Price,* 2:15b-17a.

8. Ibid., 2:19.

9. Ibid., 2:18-19.

10. For a more detailed picture of the conflicts in the story, see *Journal of Discourses* 2:196-197; 6:29,335; 10:127; 12:333-334; 13:65-66,294,324; 18:239; 20:167; 14:261-262; the *Millenial Star* 3:53,71; and *Times and Seasons* 3:749,753.

11. A thorough discussion of this matter is in *The Maze of Mormonism.*

12. Tract published by the Church of Jesus Christ of Latter-day Saints, quoted from the *Examiner,* January 1952, pp. 21-22.

13. Walter Martin, *The Maze of Mormonism,* pp. 329-332.

14. James E. Talmage, *The Articles of Faith* (Salt Lake City: The Church of Jesus Christ of Latter-day Saints, 1974), pp. 7, 457. All three "sacred" books have undergone literally thousands of changes. The *Pearl of Great Price* and *Doctrine and Covenants* have parts which are almost unrecognizable when compared with the original editions. I have maintained for more than twenty-five years that the *Book of Mormon* was taken from the novel *Manuscript Found* stolen by early Mormon leader Sidney Rigdon from its rightful author, Solomon Spalding (see note 1). The evidence, presented in *Who Really Wrote the Book of Mormon?* (Ventura, CA: Vision House, 1977), is convincing.

15. Brigham Young, *Journal of Discourses* 1:50. Some contemporary Mormon apologists argue that Young may have mentioned such teachings and may even have taught them, but that they were never interpreted or authorized as such by the church. However, Mormon President Wilford Woodruff confirmed it as Young's doctrine (*Journal of Wilford Woodruff,* April 10, 1852). Young himself declared that this teaching about Adam-God was revealed by God (*Deseret News,* June 18, 1873). Recently the Mormon church officially rejected the Adam-God doctrine of Young and his contemporaries, although refusing to admit that he had ever taught such a thing! The fact remains that the inspired president of the Mormon church claimed at the time of his revelations, that God had told him Adam was our God.

16. Joseph Smith, *Doctrine and Covenants,* 130:22.

17. B. Young, *Journal of Discourses,* 1:50.

18. James E. Talmage, *The Articles of Faith,* p. 480.

19. John Taylor, *The Mediation and Atonement* (Salt Lake City: The Church of Jesus Christ of Latter-day Saints, n.d.), pp. 170, 177-178.

20. A former Mormon leader, Lorenzo Snow, once said: "As man is, God once was—As God is, man may become" [quoted in Milton R. Hunter, *The Gospel Through the Ages* (Salt Lake City: Stevens and Wallis, Inc., 1945), p. 113].

four
The Mind Science and Healing Cults

The Bible gives us a trustworthy test for evaluating the claims of the mind science or gnostic cults. First John 4:1-3 not only commands us to test the spirits, but also gives us an example of a "false spirit": "Beloved, believe not every spirit, but try the spirits whether they are of God: because many false prophets are gone out into the world. Hereby know ye the Spirit of God: Every spirit that confesseth that Jesus Christ is come in the flesh is of God: and every spirit that confesseth not that Jesus Christ is come in the flesh is not of God: and this is that spirit of antichrist, whereof ye have heard that it should come; and even now already is it in the world."

The apostle John goes on in chapter 5 to give another distinguishing mark of the false prophets:

"Whosoever believeth that Jesus is the Christ is born of God: and every one that loveth him that begat loveth him also that is begotten of him" (v. 1).

The mind science cults always deny both that Jesus Christ was, as the Gospel of John declares, God the Word made flesh (John 1:1,14) and that the man Jesus is the Christ. Rather, the mind science cults, patterned after their ancient gnostic predecessors, denigrate the material world and deny the all-important incarnation of our Lord. The most distinguishing false teaching of the mind science cults (including Christian Science, founded by Mary Baker Eddy; Unity School of Christianity, founded by Charles and Myrtle Fillmore; Religious Science/Science of Mind, founded by Ernest Holmes; and their variations and offshoots) is that they *all* deny that Jesus *is* the Christ. They all distinguish between Jesus, identified as a man, and the Christ, or the Christ Principle, that power or energy of divinity which rested upon the man or was manifested through the man Jesus. In our brief review of the modern gnostic cults (whose combined membership estimated at around seven million is probably the largest of any of the cultic systems in America today) we will concentrate on this false doctrine, reviewing how Christian Science and Unity deny the incarnation, and reviewing the biblical injunctions against such heresy.

Today's mind science cults are not the first to promote such ideas. In fact, gnostic ideas flourished during New Testament times, and New Testament writers Paul and John wrote in direct opposition to gnostic ideas which were threatening new Christian communities. We have seen above what John wrote in his first Epistle, 1 John. Shortly we will review some of his anti-gnostic ideas in his Gospel and Paul's refutations of gnostic ideas in his letters to the Colossians and the Ephesians.

Gnosticism is a complex system, almost more philosophical than religious. All gnostic teaching is based on the philosophical presupposition that the Ultimate Reality (their God concept) is pure and unapproachable Spirit and that the material world is the opposite of that divinity. Some gnostics deny that the material world has any existence at all, but is only illusory (so believes Christian Science). Some gnostics admit that the material world exists, but state that it is transitory, corrupt, and will eventually be consumed by the Divine Spirit (so believes Unity). All gnostics believe that it is impossible for God (as defined above) to have any direct contact with the base material world. Instead, gnostics postulate "emanations" from God which become successively less spirit and more material. Some gnostics personalize these emanations as "angels," believing that God and His will can be known only through the successive messages of these angels. We will see how important this idea is when we discuss the biblical and Christian doctrine of the incarnation.

The entire tenor of the Bible, Old and New Testaments, is against these basic presuppositions of gnosticism. In fact, the Gospel of John opens with doctrine diametrically opposed to the claims of gnosticism. John tells us that Jesus Christ was not just man, recipient of a divine emanation, or one on whom some "Christ Presence" rested. On the contrary, John tells us: "In the beginning was the Word, and the Word was with God, and the Word was God. The same was in the beginning with God . . . . And the Word was made flesh, and dwelt among us, (and we beheld his glory, the glory as of the only begotten of the Father,) full of grace and truth" (John 1:1-2,14).

As we explore the world of gnosticism, the world of the mind sciences, we will see its specific deviations from biblical truth and will document, from Scripture, God's responses to such aberrations.

CHRISTIAN SCIENCE

The religion of Christian Science has, since its earliest beginnings, presented a challenge to orthodox Christianity by denying biblical doctrine and pointing to its supposed power to heal as validation of its heretical teachings. Within the ranks of the Christian Science church today are to be found many thousands of former churchgoing folk who held membership in our major Protestant denominations (present Christian Science membership is around four hundred thousand). Although for many years the Christian Science church has grown steadily, in recent years membership has dropped markedly. The number of its churches and practitioners is in a long-term decline. In an article by *Los Angeles Times* religion writer John Dart (October 31, 1976), we read, "In California, the state with the largest Christian Scientist population, the listed practitioners have dropped from more than 2,200 in 1946 to about 1,100 today." According to the January 1979 *Christian Science Journal,* nine Christian Science churches and societies folded in California in 1978. This continued a trend which saw 383 California churches and societies in 1966 and in 1978 only 343 churches and societies. However, the threat of Christian Science to true Christianity is still very real, since almost all of the rapidly growing contemporary gnostic cults can be traced in a more or less direct line from the heresies of Christian Science founder Mary Baker Eddy. Many are involved in the mind sciences today mainly because at one time in their lives they underwent some type of "healing" which they attributed to the "revelation" given by Mary Baker Eddy, as found in her textbook *Science and Health with*

Key to the Scriptures.

Christian Science has offered to these people a sanctuary from the preaching of the gospel of Christ, which points out the terrible reality of sin and evil in man's nature and strips from the soul every vestige of self-righteousness. Mrs. Eddy's religion, on the other hand, offers no such hazards, denying as it does the existence of evil, sin, sickness, and even death itself.

The average Christian Scientist can well afford, therefore, to remain oblivious to the necessity of repentance from sin and faith in the blood of the Lamb, which Mrs. Eddy discounts entirely in its vicarious biblical application.[1]

The theology of Christian Science prohibits any acceptance whatsoever of the vicarious atonement of our Lord, and blatantly denies eternal retribution for those who willfully reject Jesus Christ as "the Lamb of God, which taketh away the sin of the world" (John 1:29).[2]

The Christian Scientists, like the other mind science cults, deny the all-sufficiency and inerrancy of the Bible, Old and New Testaments. Instead, the mind science cults hold the writings of their founders/leaders as a better and more accurate revelation than that found in the Bible. Christian Science considers Mrs. Eddy's textbook and other writings as virtually infallible.

With these thoughts in mind, let us now consider the history, theology, and peculiarities of Christian Science, the first of the heretical modern gnostic cults, all of which deny the biblical and evangelical Christian faith.

Mary Ann Morse Baker, the future Mrs. Eddy, was born in Bow, New Hampshire, in the year 1821 to Mark and Abigail Baker, hearty farmers and staunch Congregationalists by religion. During her childhood Mary Baker was quite sickly and given to fits of depression and extreme temper, which made life with her at that period almost intolerable.[3]

In the year 1843, at the age of twenty-two, Mary Baker married George W. Glover, the first of her three husbands and most probably her one great love. The first marriage of Mary Baker ended almost as soon as it began, for less than seven months later George W. Glover was stricken with yellow fever while on a trip to Wilmington, North Carolina, from the newlyweds' home in Charleston, South Carolina. The death of her husband prostrated the young wife, who was then about to bear her first and only child, George W. Glover, Jr. Later in life, Mrs. Eddy adopted another son, Dr. E. J. Foster Eddy, who at one time took charge of publishing her book *Science and Health.*

After the death of George Glover, Sr., the widowed Mary Glover returned to her father's home in Tilton, New Hampshire where her child was born and subsequently reared.

The second marriage of Mary Baker Glover was contracted almost ten years to the day after her first husband died, and was to Dr. Daniel Patterson, a handsome and amorous dentist whom she later divorced, charging adultery, though such was never conclusively proved.

The final marriage of Mary Baker Glover Patterson was to one Asa G. Eddy, a student of Christian Science, whose meek temperament led him to acquiesce to her every whim with perfect obedience. The last marriage of Mrs. Eddy strangely enough caused her more trouble publicly than either of the previous two, for upon the death of Asa, Mrs. Eddy claimed that he had been killed by arsenic poisoning.[4]

This rather strange diagnosis aroused the medical profession considerably, and she was denounced for even entertaining such a diagnosis. Mrs. Eddy's chief witness for her diagnostic efforts was "Dr." C. J. Eastman, dean of the Bellevue Medical College, who was later exposed as a quack and sentenced to prison, and his college was closed. "Dr." Eastman's opinions were therefore utterly worthless; as the autopsy on Asa disclosed, he died of a chronic heart condition just as Dr. Rufus Noyes, the attending physician, had originally declared.[5]

Mary Baker Eddy did not arrive on the religious scene with a wholly new revelation. As we mentioned in the beginning of this chapter, Christian Science and the other modern mind science cults are revivals of the ancient gnostic heresies which were soundly condemned during the first centuries of the Christian Church. However, Mrs. Eddy did not even take her "revelation" directly from those ancient gnostics. Instead, she is indebted to a nineteenth-century mesmerist-turned-mind-scientist, Phineas Parkhurst Quimby. "Dr." Quimby wrote, taught, and practiced all of the essential features of Christian Science doctrine, and called his practice "the science of Christ" and "Christian Science," almost a decade before Mrs. Eddy's new "revelation" was first published in *Science and Health*.[6] It was no coincidence that Mrs. Eddy came up with the "Quimby Method" years later. Mrs. Eddy was "healed" by Quimby in 1862,[7] was his student for a number of years, possessed, studied, and annotated some of his manuscripts,[8] and eulogized him as one "who Healed with the Truth that Christ Taught in Contradistinction to All Isms."[9] She declared that "P. P. Quimby . . . heals as never man healed since Christ."[10]

In later years, however, when Mrs. Eddy was charged with pirating Quimby's ideas to form the basis of her book *Science and Health* (1875), she spoke of Quimby in anything but complimentary terms, referring to him as "illiterate" and "a very unlearned man," etc., though she admitted privately to her literary adviser, the Reverend J. H. Wiggin, that the charges were essentially true.[11]

That Mrs. Eddy had access to Quimby's ideas and even owned a copy of one of his manuscripts (*Questions and Answers*), which contains changes in her own handwriting, no competent scholar denies. For a comparison of this manuscript with Mrs. Eddy's writings, see the *New York Times,* July 10, 1904.

The attempt, therefore, to discredit Quimby's influence upon Mrs. Eddy and her textbook has never been relaxed by the Christian Scientists and their supporters, proof of which is found in Sibyl Wilbur's biography of Mrs. Eddy,[12] the official publication of the church, and Norman Beasley's *The Cross and the Crown,* wherein Quimby is dismissed, all evidence to the contrary. The facts, however, still remain, and any fair-minded person will have little difficulty in ascertaining that Mrs. Eddy is not "the discoverer and founder of a new religion" at all, but merely the instrument which expanded and recognized the teachings of P. P. Quimby, the father of Christian Science.

Miraculous healing is widely advertised by Christian Science and the other mind sciences. Because hope of healing is a great incentive for people to join one of the mind science cults, it is important that we examine such claims of supernatural healing power. We shall use Mrs. Eddy and her Christian Science as representative of the "healing power" of the mind sciences. While their claims are sweeping and grandiose (as were those of Mrs. Eddy), they are consistently unable to deliver on their promises. For example, in the *New York Sun* of December 19, 1898, Mrs. Eddy boldly "challenged the world to disprove" that she had healed "consumption in the last stages . . . malignant tubercular diptheria . . . carious bones . . . a cancer that had so eaten the flesh of the neck as to expose the jugular vein . . . . " This challenge was quickly accepted by Dr. Charles A. L. Reed of Cincinnati (later president of the American Medical Association) in the *Sun* of January 1, 1899. Dr. Reed offered to present Mrs. Eddy with similar cases and "if she, by her Christian Science, shall cure any one of them, I shall proclaim her omnipotence from the housetops; and, if she shall cure all, or even half of them, I shall cheerfully crawl upon my hands and knees that I may but touch the hem of her walking-dress." Dr. Reed even offered to make arrangements for Mrs. Eddy to "heal at one visit" identical cases then under treatment at Bellevue or "some other New York Hospital" to spare her the fatigue of a trip to Cincinnati. The eminent physician completed his offer in the following words, which are noted for their fair analysis of the issue then at hand:

> If Mrs. Eddy will accept this challenge and cure one or more of the cases, she will thereby demonstrate that she may be something more than either a conscienceless speculator on human credulity or an unfortunate victim of egotistic alienation.

Mrs. Eddy never accepted Dr. Reed's offer, nor did she care to discuss the matter at length again, and for a very good reason later revealed during the cross-examination of Mr. Alfred Farlow[13] by F. W. Peabody, noted Boston lawyer and implacable enemy of Christian Science. Mr. Farlow was at the time chairman of the Publication Committee of the Christian Science church and president of the Mother Church in Boston, and was therefore in an excellent position to know the facts about Mrs. Eddy. Yet he swore under oath that he did not know of *any* healing ever having been made by Mrs. Eddy of *any* organic disease in her entire life, except *stiff leg*!

These facts, then, show quite plainly that Mrs. Eddy's claim to divine healing power was indeed evidence of a most vital truth deadly to the cause of Christian Science—the truth that Mrs. Eddy never healed as she claimed, could not heal properly diagnosed organic diseases when challenged, and dared not put her vaunted powers to an open test. Let those who enter Christian Science take with them this warning in the light of these facts: Mary Baker Eddy did not heal, as her zealous disciples maintain; in fact, she made use of medical care herself in later years, both doctors and dentists, and even utilized morphine as a painkiller for her various "attacks."[14]

There is very little doubt in my mind that a great many "cures" recorded by the Christian Science church are psychosomatic in nature, induced by suggestion and a concentrated form of psychotherapy which at times has the appearance of a miraculous intervention. As Dr. David Davis of Bellevue has said, "What has been induced by suggestion can be removed by suggestion," and this is doubtless true of some of the accomplishments of Mrs. Eddy's practitioners.

Similarly, there are seemingly verifiable cases of healings by Christian Scientists, of both fellow Scientists and non-Scientists, which apparently defy contradiction and are, I believe, a direct fulfillment of what Christ warned us of in His famous discourse as recorded in Matthew 7:15-23. Contrary to popular opinion, healing is not always a sign of divine favor, and never so when it is effected by those who deny the authority of the Scriptures and the very Christ in whose name they claim to heal. The Bible clearly teaches that Satan's emissaries can also duplicate miracles, as in the case of Moses and the Egyptian magicians as recorded in the book of Exodus (7:11,22; 8:7,18). Wonders do not always mean that God is working, for He works only to the glory of Jesus Christ and in perfect accord with biblical doctrine. The same kinds of miracles spoken of in a godly sense in Hebrews 2:4 are counterfeited by Satan in 2 Thessalonians 2:9. Mind scientists, modern-day gnostics, deny both the authority of Scripture and the deity of Christ, and therefore it is of them, among others, that Jesus warned His disciples and us. Let us therefore be diligent lest we be deceived by those whose powers are after the workings of Satan, with "signs and [lying] wonders."

UNITY SCHOOL OF CHRISTIANITY

Shortly we shall review systematically gnostic heresy (using Christian Science as representative of modern gnosticism or mind science) and compare its perversions of essential doctrine with the teachings of the Bible. Before that, however, we will present a summary of the history and practices of the largest modern mind science cult, the Unity School of Christianity.

Charles and Myrtle Fillmore first promulgated their "new" revelation in 1889. Unity School of Christianity (its various name changes are discussed, along with extensive history of Unity, in my text *The Kingdom of the Cults*) borrowed extensively from Mary Baker Eddy's Christian Science. The cult began with a small home Bible study, which emphasized the power of the mind to heal and the "truth" that God was ultimately Impersonal Mind.

Today Unity is the largest and fastest growing of the gnostic cults. It concentrates on propaganda through literature and radio and television. Its sugarcoated and doctrinally nebulous periodicals have been accepted (usually unwittingly) by many innocent Christians. Some

Protestant churches even subscribe to multiple issues of Unity periodicals!

The underlying themes of Unity publications is that no problem is insoluble if one practices Unity's tenets faithfully, and Unity offers not only health and happiness but financial security as well. Coupled with the appeal of such doctrinal aberrations as denial of hell, assertion of reincarnation, and the promise that each of us is equal to Jesus Christ, such themes are very attractive. Unfortunately, they are deceptive counterfeits by Satan of the truths of the gospel, as we shall see.

Today, the Unity School of Christianity has 161 centers in 40 states and foreign countries, 314 ministers and practitioners (no statistics on individual membership are available), many well-edited magazines, a huge printing operation at headquarters in Unity Village, near Lee Summit and Kansas City, Missouri, a Sunday-School quarterly (*Wee Wisdom*), and a restaurant for vegetarians that has no equal for either variety or quality.

Charles Fillmore supervised the entire facilities of his huge empire until death claimed him in 1948 in his nineties. Myrtle Fillmore, his wife, partner, and cofounder of Unity, died in 1931. However, the aging prophet of eternal youth subsequently married Cora Dedrick, his secretary, who survived him as well as some of his children and grandchildren. His son Lowell is now head of the Unity Operation.

The literature of Unity Christianity is published in the best taste; the paper is good and the bindings are excellent. The style of writing is also very appealing, since it makes much use of biblical references and illustrations. Unfortunately, the average person who either listens to a Unity broadcast or reads from its numerous publications doubtless believes Unity to be a form of Christian theology. But it is not, in any sane use of the word, as I shall now demonstrate conclusively from its own written propaganda.

The Trinity

"The Father is Principle, the Son is that Principle revealed in a creative plan, the Holy Spirit is the executive power of both Father and Son carrying out the creative plan."[15]

For Unity, then, the God of the Bible is an impersonal "It," a Principle, Supreme Intelligence, Divine Mind, etc. In no sense, they teach, is He a personal Being.

The Bible

While Unity pays lip service to the divine inspiration of the Bible, their loyalty to it is fickle. Where it suits their purposes it is quoted, albeit usually out of context. Where it contradicts Unity doctrine it is either dismissed or "reinterpreted." An example of such "reinterpretation" is a "metaphysical interpretation" of Psalm 23, written by Charles Fillmore in his *Prosperity* (p. 60):

> The Lord is my banker; my credit is good. He maketh me to lie down in the consciousness of omnipotent abundance. He giveth me the key to His strongbox. He restoreth my faith in His riches. He guideth me in the paths of prosperity for His name's sake. Yes, though I walk through the very shadow of debt, I shall fear no evil, for Thou art with me; Thy silver and gold, they secure me. Thou preparest a way for me in the presence of the collector; Thou fillest my wallet with plenty; my measure runneth over. Surely, goodness and plenty will follow me all the days of my life; and I shall do business in the name of the Lord forever.

Any reasonably intelligent individual cannot fail to see that this interpretation by Fillmore is a direct and absolute perversion of David's psalm, which stresses dependence upon a personal God, not a glorified impersonal banker.

Jesus Christ

Unity denies the complete and absolute deity of Jesus of Nazareth and insists instead that He and "the Christ, the spiritual identity of Jesus," are two separate entities.

> The Bible says that God so loved the world that he gave his only begotten Son, but the Bible does not here refer to Jesus of Nazareth, the outer man; it refers to the Christ, the spiritual identity of Jesus, whom he acknowledged in all his ways, and brought forth into his outer, until even the flesh of his body was lifted up, purified, spiritualized, and redeemed. Thus he became Jesus Christ, the Word made flesh. And we are to follow into this perfect state and become like him, for in each of us is the Christ, the only begotten Son. We can, through Jesus Christ, our Redeemer and Example, bring forth the Christ within us, the true self of all men, and be made perfect even as our Father in heaven is perfect, as Jesus Christ commanded his followers to be.[16]

The Bible declares that the eternal Word of God (John 1:1) became Man in Jesus of Nazareth (John 1:14) and that He never ceased to be the Deity—that He was and ever shall be God (Phil. 2:6-8; Col. 2:9; John 8:58; Rev. 1:8-18; etc.). Jesus Christ was not Jesus *and* Christ, as the gnostics and Unity cultists would have us believe; rather, He was the God-Man, two natures but one divine person immutable forever.

The interested reader will also observe that Unity reduces the Lord Jesus Christ to the level of a mere man who had within Him "the perfect Christ idea," and "that same Christ idea is in every man." Thus it is taught by Unity that all men are miniature Christs, sharing in His nature and power. Should any doubt this assertion, we quote Unity's own literature to substantiate our contention: "Jesus was able to say, 'All authority has been given to me in heaven and on earth'—we, too, can say truthfully that this authority has been given to us."[17]

The Atonement and the Resurrection

Unity must deny the biblical doctrines of the atonement and the resurrection since it teaches clearly, "There is no sin, sickness, or death."[18]

Opposed to this outright denial of sin's existence we find the plain declarations of Scripture: "All have sinned, and come short of the glory of God" (Rom. 3:23); "All unrighteousness is sin" (1 John 5:17); "If we say that we have no sin, we deceive ourselves, and the truth is not in us" (1 John 1:8).

In sharp contrast to this scriptural picture of the atonement, the Unity view projects itself in unmistakable language: "The atonement is the union of man with God the Father, in Christ. Stating it in terms of mind, we should say that the atonement is the at-one-ment or agreement of reconciliation of man's mind with Divine Mind through the super-consciousness of Christ mind."[19]

The original Hebrew and Greek languages of the Bible leave no room for the chopping apart of syllables, such as Unity practices on the English translations; therefore, linguistically speaking, the entire view they promulgate, based on a purely arbitrary dissection of the term *atonement,* is a monstrous farce hardly worthy of refutation.

Respecting the doctrine of the resurrection of our Lord, and of all men for that matter, it should be noted that Unity believes in and boldly teaches reincarnation in place of resurrection, as this quotation from their statement of faith amply demonstrates: "We believe that the dissolution of spirit, soul and body, caused by death, is annulled by rebirth of the same spirit and soul in another body here on earth. We believe the repeated incarnations of man to be a merciful provision of our loving Father to the end that all may have opportunity to attain immortality through regeneration as did Jesus. 'This corruptible must put on incorruption.' "[20]

One may see in this thoroughly pagan view that Unity, Theosophy, Hinduism, Buddhism, and countless other Oriental philosophies go hand-in-hand down the primrose path of reincarnation, which the Scriptures flatly contradict by declaring for the Christian, "To be absent from the body [is] to be present with the Lord" (2 Cor. 5:8); and for the non-Christian, "He that believeth not the Son shall not see life; but the wrath of God abideth on him" (John 3:36). Innumerable passages of Scripture belie the concept of reincarnation, which brands Unity irrevocably as a dangerous non-Christian cult.

In completing this outline of the mind science cults it is my conviction that a series of quotations from Christian Science sources will prove helpful to the average reader who has neither the time nor possibly the inclination to hunt up all the pertinent facts relative to the nearly identical doctrines of the various gnostic cults.

To enable such readers to have this valuable source material at their fingertips, I have listed sixteen of the major doctrines of Christianity, together with contradictory quotations taken directly from Mrs. Eddy's writings. These comparisons will, I believe, provide sufficient documentation should a dispute ever arise concerning the classification of any of the mind science cults as a Christian religion.

Inspiration of the Bible

1. Referring to Genesis 2:7: "Is this addition to His creation real or unreal? Is it the truth—, or is it a lie concerning man and God?

It must be a lie, . . . " (*Science and Health,* p. 524).

2. " . . . the manifest mistakes in the ancient versions; the thirty thousand different readings in the Old Testament, and the three hundred thousand in the New,—these facts show how a mortal and material sense stole into the divine record, with its own hue darkening to some extent the inspired pages" (ibid., p. 139).

The Doctrine of the Trinity and the Deity of Christ

1. "The theory of three persons in one God (that is, a personal Trinity or Tri-unity) suggests polytheism, rather than the one ever-present I AM" (ibid., p. 152).

2. "The Christian who believes in the First Commandment is a monotheist. Thus he virtually unites with the Jew's belief in one God, and recognizes that Jesus Christ is not God as Jesus Himself declared, but is the Son of God" (ibid., p. 361).

3. "The spiritual Christ was infallible; Jesus, as material manhood, was not Christ" (*Miscellaneous Writings,* p. 84).

The Doctrine of God and the Holy Spirit

1. "The Jewish tribal Jehovah was a man-projected God, liable to wrath, repentance, and human change-

ableness" (*Science and Health,* p. 140).

2. "God. The great I AM; the all-knowing, all-seeing, all-acting, all-wise, all-loving, and eternal; Principle; Mind; Soul; Spirit; Life; Truth; Love; all substance; intelligence" (ibid., p. 587).

3. "1. God is All-in-all. 2. God is good. Good is Mind. 3. God, Spirit, being all, nothing is matter . . . GOD: Divine Principle, Life, Truth, Love, Soul, Spirit, Mind" (ibid., pp. 113, 115).

The Virgin Birth of Christ

1. "A portion of God could not enter man; neither could God's fullness be reflected by a single man, else God would be manifestly finite, lose the deific character, and become less than God" (ibid., p. 336).

2. "The Virgin-mother conceived this idea of God, and gave to her ideal the name of Jesus—that is, Joshua, or Saviour.

"The illumination of Mary's spiritual sense put to silence material law and its order of generation, and brought forth her child by the revelation of Truth, demonstrating God as the Father of men. The Holy Ghost, or divine Spirit, overshadowed the pure sense of the Virgin-mother with the full recognition that being is Spirit. The Christ dwelt forever an idea in the bosom of God, the divine Principle of the man Jesus, and woman perceived this spiritual idea, though at first faintly developed.

"Jesus was the offspring of Mary's self-conscious communion with God" (ibid., pp. 29-30).

The Doctrine of Miracles

1. "The sick are not healed merely by declaring there is no sickness, but by knowing that there is none" (ibid., p. 447).

2. "Sickness is part of the error which Truth casts

out. Error will not expel error. Christian Science is the law of Truth, which heals the sick on the basis of the one Mind or God. It can heal in no other way, since the human, mortal mind so-called is not a healer, but causes the belief in disease" (ibid., p. 482).

3. "The so-called miracles contained in Holy Writ are neither supernatural or preternatural . . . Jesus regarded good as the normal state of mind and evil as the abnormal . . . . The so-called pains and pleasures of matter were alike unreal to Jesus; for He regarded matter as only a vagary of mortal belief, and subdued it with this understanding" (*Miscellaneous Writings,* pp. 200-201).

The Atonement of Jesus Christ

1. "The material blood of Jesus was no more efficacious to cleanse from sin when it was shed upon 'the accursed tree,' than when it was flowing in his veins, as he went daily about his Father's business" (*Science and Health,* p. 25).

2. "The real atonement—so infinitely beyond the heathen conception that God requires human blood to propitiate His justice and bring His mercy—needs to be understood" (*No and Yes,* p. 34).

3. "One sacrifice, however great, is insufficient to pay the debt of sin" (*Science and Health,* p. 23).

The Death and Resurrection of Christ

1. "Jesus' students, not sufficiently advanced fully to understand their Master's triumph, did not perform many wonderful works, until they saw him after his crucifixion and learned that He had not died" (ibid., pp. 45-46).

2. "His disciples believed Jesus to be dead while he was hidden in the sepulchre, whereas he was alive, demonstrating within the narrow tomb the power of Spirit to

overrule mortal, material sense" (ibid., p. 44).

The Ascension and Second Coming of Christ

1. " . . . until he himself ascended,—or, in other words, rose even higher in the understanding of Spirit, God . . . . Jesus' unchanged physical condition after what seemed to be death was followed by his exaltation above all material conditions; and this exaltation explained his ascension . . . . In his final demonstration, called the ascension, which closed the earthly record of Jesus, he rose above the physical knowledge of his disciples, and the material senses saw him no more" (ibid., p. 46).

Satan and the Existence of Evil

1. "Hence, evil is but an illusion, and it has no real basis. Evil is a false belief. God is not its author. The suppositious parent of evil is a lie" (ibid., p. 480).

2. "DEVIL. Evil; a lie; error; neither corporeality nor mind; the opposite of Truth; a belief in sin, sickness, and death; animal magnetism or hypnotism; the lust of the flesh, . . . " (ibid., p. 584).

The Nature and Existence of Hell

1. "The sinner makes his own hell by doing evil, and the saint his own heaven by doing right" (ibid., p. 266).

2. "The advanced psychist knows that this hell is mental, not material, and that the Christian has no part in it" (*The First Church of Christ, Scientist, and Miscellany*, p. 160).

The Kingdom of Heaven—Its Reality and Significance

1. "HEAVEN. Harmony; the reign of the Spirit; government by divine Principle; spirituality; bliss; the atmo-

sphere of Soul" (*Science and Health,* p. 587).

2. "Heaven is not a locality, but a divine state of Mind in which all the manifestations of Mind are harmonious and immortal, because sin is not there and man is found having no righteousness of his own, but in possession of 'the mind of the Lord,' as the Scripture says" (ibid., p. 291).

The Doctrine of Eternal Salvation

1. "Man as God's idea is already saved with an everlasting salvation" (*Miscellaneous Writings,* p. 261).

2. "SALVATION. Life, Truth, and Love understood and demonstrated as supreme over all; sin, sickness, and death destroyed" (*Science and Health,* p. 593).

The Doctrine of Prayer

1. "Prayer can neither change God, nor bring his designs into mortal modes—I have no objection to audible prayer of the right kind; but inaudible is more effectual" (*No and Yes,* pp. 48, 50).

2. "If prayer nourishes the belief that sin is cancelled, and that man is made better merely by praying, prayer is an evil. He grows worse who continues in sin because he fancies himself forgiven" (*Science and Health,* p. 4).

The Creation of Matter and Its Reality

1. "There is . . . no intelligent sin, evil mind or matter; and this is the only true philosophy and realism" (*No and Yes,* p. 47).

2. "There is no life, truth, intelligence nor substance in matter. All is infinite Mind and its infinite manifestation, for God is All-in-all" (*Science and Health,* p. 468).

Man, the Soul, His True Nature and Destiny

1. "Man is not matter; . . . . Man is spiritual and per-

fect; and because he is spiritual and perfect, he must be so understood in Christian Science. Man is idea, the image, of Love; he is not physique" (ibid., p. 475).

2. "Man is God's image and likeness; whatever is possible to God, is possible to man as God's reflection" (*Miscellaneous Writings,* p. 183).

3. "The great spiritual fact must be brought out that man *is,* not *shall be,* perfect and immortal" (*Science and Health,* p. 428).

The Existence of Sin, Sickness, and Death

1. "Do not believe in any supposed necessity for sin, disease, or death, knowing (as you ought to know) that God never requires obedience to a so-called material law, for no such law exists. The belief in sin and death is destroyed by the law of God, which is the law of Life instead of death, of harmony instead of discord, of Spirit instead of flesh" (ibid., p. 253).

2. "DEVIL. Evil; a lie; error; neither corporeality nor mind; the opposite of Truth; a belief in sin, sickness, and death; animal magnetism or hypnotism; the lust of the flesh, . . . " (ibid., p. 584).

3. "Therefore the only reality of sin, sickness, or death is the awful fact that unrealities seem real to human, erring belief, until God strips off their disguise. They are not true, because they are not of God" (ibid., p. 472).

Biblical Texts Helpful in Refuting Mind Science (Gnostic) Theology

The Authority of the Bible: Psalm 119:140; Isaiah 40:8; Matthew 24:35; John 10:35; 17:17; 2 Timothy 3:16.

The Trinity and the Death of Christ: Genesis 1:26; 11:7; 18:1-33; Exodus 3:14; Isaiah 9:6; John 1:1, 14; 8:58; Colossians 1:15; 2:9; Hebrews 1:3; Revelation 1:7-8, 16.

The Personality of the Holy Spirit: Luke 12:12; John 16:7,8; Acts 5:1-5; 13:2.

The Virgin Birth and Miracles of Jesus: Isaiah 7:14; 9:6; Micah 5:2; Matthew 1:18-25; 8:14-15, 26-27; 9:2, 6-7, 27-30; Mark 1:32-34; Luke 1:30-38; John 2:1-11; 6:10-14.

The Atonement, Death, and Resurrection of Christ: Exodus 12:13; Leviticus 17:11; Psalm 22; Isaiah 53; Daniel 9:26; Matthew 26:28; 28:5-7; Luke 24:39; John 1:29; 19:33; Romans 5:6-8; Ephesians 1:7; Colossians 1:20.

The Doctrine of Eternal Retribution: Matthew 13:42, 50; 22:13; Mark 9:44, 46, 48; Luke 3:17; Revelation 20:10.

The Doctrine of Christian Prayer: Matthew 6:5-15; 7:7-11; Luke 18:1; Philippians 4:6; 1 Thessalonians 5:17.

The Doctrine of Sin: Romans 3:23; 6:23; 1 John 1:10; 3:4; 5:17.

Notes

1. *Science and Health with Key to the Scriptures,* p. 334. (References are always to the 1971 edition unless otherwise noted.)

2. Ibid., p. 476.

3. Georgine Milmine, *The Life of Mary Baker G. Eddy and the History of Christian Science* (New York: Doubleday and Company, Inc., 1909, 1937), pp. 3, 12-13.

4. See the *Boston Post,* June 5, 1882.

5. See my booklet *Christian Science* (Minneapolis: Bethany House Publishers, 1976).

6. Milmine, *Life of Mary Baker G. Eddy,* p. 52.

7. The Portland (Maine) *Courier,* November 7, 1862.

8. Milmine, *Life of Mary Baker G. Eddy,* p. 72.

9. Ibid., p. 70.

10. Ibid., p. 60.

11. See Livingstone Wright, *How Rev. Wiggin Rewrote Mrs. Eddy's Book,* p. 41.

12. Sibyl Wilbur, *The Life of Mary Baker Eddy,* pp. 93-101.

13. F.W. Peabody, *The Religio-Medical Masquerade,* p. 113.

14. Ernest Sutherland Bates and John V. Dittemore, *Mary Baker Eddy: The Truth and the Tradition* (New York: Alfred A. Knopf, Inc., 1932), pp. 41-42,

151, 445cf. *Science and Health,* p. 464.
15. *Metaphysical Bible Dictionary* (Lee's Summit, MO: Unity School of Christianity, 1962), p. 629.
16. *Unity,* vol. 57, no. 5, p. 464, and vol. 72, no. 2, p. 8.
17. *Good Business,* July 1949.
18. *Unity,* vol. 47, no. 5, p. 403.
19. *What Practical Christianity Stands For,* p. 5.
20. Unity Statement of Faith, Article 22.

five
The Occult Explosion

The mysterious world of the occult has exploded into the fastest growing religious activity in the world. Since the early 1960s occult groups and practices have gained widespread public notice, recognition and, in many instances, acceptance. Occultic practices are openly indulged in by ordinary people, and such practices range from astrology through divining, palmistry, tarot cards, and tea readings to outright witchcraft. Some estimates put the number of Americans favorably disposed to satanic and witchcraft activities at over four million. *Time* declared that over sixty million Americans were affected in some way (ranging from reading astrology columns in newspapers all the way to participating in satanic rituals) by the practices of the occult. There has been more published on the occult and its practices in the last fifteen to twenty years than was published in the previous fifty years. The challenge to the gospel presented by the explosion of the world of the occult must be answered. We shall attempt that here.

The term *occult* comes from the Latin and refers to that which is "hidden" or "secret." Occultic practices are those which are associated with Satan and his demons, known as the inhabitants of "darkness." What they do and promote, therefore, is associated with darkness and hence are "hidden" or "secret." From the very first, God warned His people to stay completely away from such practices and the followers of Satan and his demons.

In Deuteronomy God warned the Hebrew people to fix their attention on Him and to reject the occult: "The secret things belong unto the Lord our God: but those things which are revealed belong unto us and to our children for ever, that we may do all the words of this law" (Deut. 29:29). Earlier in the same book the Lord was explicit and dogmatic about occultic practices and followers, calling such things "abominations": "When thou art come into the land which the Lord thy God giveth thee, thou shalt not learn to do after the abominations of those nations. There shall not be found among you any one that maketh his son or his daughter to pass through the fire, or that useth divination, or an observer of times, or an enchanter, or a witch. Or a charmer, or a consulter with familiar spirits, or a wizard, or a necromancer. For all that do these things are an abomination unto the Lord: and because of these abominations the Lord thy God doth drive them out from before thee. Thou shalt be perfect with the Lord thy God" (Deut. 18:9-13).

The Old Testament prophets associated occultic practices with witches, fortune-tellers, idols and idol worship, and all types of sexual perversion (see, for example, Mic. 5:12-15). In the New Testament occultic practices are also seen as a works of the flesh (Gal. 5:19-20). The

Bible, then, is clear and consistent in its absolute abhorrence and rejection of all types of occultic practices.

The Bible talks of four realms or dimensions of reality. The one with which we are most familiar is the material world, including the earth and its inhabitants. Another one, which is a focus of biblical hope, is the heavenly realm, the dwelling place of God, His good angels, and those of the redeemed who have died. This realm is not material or physical and is not locatable in any geographical sense. However, it is very real and can interact, through the dynamic will of God, with the material realm we know around us.

A third realm or dimension of reality is that immaterial realm created by God as the ultimate destiny of Satan, his evil angels or demons, and those who reject everlasting life. Hell is as real as heaven and is a fitting and just "reward" for those who reject eternity with God Almighty. While the Bible uses many metaphors from our physical world to describe hell, we must remember that it is a spiritual dimension. We can quite accurately state that whatever hell is like, it entails separation from the benevolent presence of God.

The fourth dimension described in the Bible is sometimes referred to as the realm of "darkness." Ephesians 6, in the New Testament, gives us a clear picture of this powerful yet invisible world. Paul reminds the Christians of their power in the Lord and warns them of the spiritual battle in this realm of darkness: "Finally, my brethren, be strong in the Lord, and in the power of his might. Put on the whole armour of God, that ye may be able to stand against the wiles of the devil. For we wrestle not against flesh and blood, but against principalities, against powers, against the rulers of the darkness of this world, against spiritual wickedness in high places. Wherefore take unto you the whole armour of God, that ye may be able to withstand in the evil day, and having done all, to stand" (Eph. 6:10-13).

It is this realm of darkness that produces and sustains the occult explosion we see around us today. It is powerful and deadly to those who are not protected by the "armour" of God.

In this chapter we will survey the world of the occult, using the occultic movement known as *spiritism* (sometimes erroneously called "spiritualism") as representative of the earthly manifestations of this dark kingdom. Our survey would not be complete unless we conclude it with a clear declaration of the power of the Lord Jesus Christ to redeem those caught in occultism, and to protect those who belong to Him.

HISTORY OF SPIRITISM

Of all the religious source books in the world, the Bible unquestionably gives the history of spiritism in a most concise and dependable form.[1] As far back as the book of Exodus, the Scriptures reveal that the ancient Egyptians were practitioners of occultism, magic, sorcery, and necromancy, which they employed to duplicate the miracles of Moses when that great servant of the Lord appeared before Pharaoh (Exod. 7:11,22; 8:18; etc.).

The attitude of God toward those who practiced such forbidden sins is also clearly outlined in Scripture, for the Lord ordered the death penalty for all sorcerers (Hebrew, *mekashshetah*), as recorded in Exodus 22:18 and Leviticus 20:27, to cite two concrete instances. The Old Testament also named among those cursed by Jehovah persons consorting with "familiar spirits" and "wizards" (see Lev. 19:31 and 20:6) as well as "necromancers" (Deut. 18:10-11), etc.

In company with these violators of divine command,

Daniel the prophet speaks often of the "magicians" (Hebrew, *hartummim*), "sorcerers," "soothsayers" and "astrologers" (Dan. 1:20; 2:2,10,27; 4:7; 5:7; etc.) who specialized along with the Chaldeans in the art of interpreting dreams and visions. The prophet Isaiah (8:19; 19:3) also speaks of such ancient spiritists as casting "sorceries" upon Israel (Isa. 47:9), and King Saul before his apostasy drove such practitioners from Israel (1 Sam. 28:3,9), as did the righteous King Josiah after him (2 Kings 23:24-25).

The Scriptures likewise bear record that King Manasseh's downfall came about as a result of his delving into spiritism (2 Kings 21:6; 2 Chron. 33:6), and his ensuing practice of idolatry in defiance of the command of Jehovah. The Bible then presents a devastating resumé of man's forbidden desire to uncover the hidden spiritual mysteries of the universe, even if "witchcraft" (2 Kings 9:22; Mic. 5:12; Nah. 3:4), "divination" (1 Sam. 15:23), or "enchantments" (2 Chron. 33:6) must be employed to further his unholy quest. The Egyptians (Exod. 8:18), Babylonians, Chaldeans (Dan. 2:2), and Canaanites (Lev. 19:31), Scripture tells us, all practiced spiritism.

Today in the United States there are said to be in excess of 164 "churches" actively associated with the National Spiritualist Association, with 144 ordained clergy and 5,168 Sunday or Sabbath Schools.[2] In South America there are over eight million practicing spritists, despite the power of the Roman Catholic Church there. Many South American Roman Catholics even combine spiritistic practices with superstitious interpretations of Catholicism.

Spiritism today is much more sophisticated than it was during the early years in the United States and Great Britain when Sir Arthur Conan Doyle—creator of Sherlock Holmes, William James—noted philosopher, psy-

chologist, and psychic research expert, and Sir Oliver
Lodge—British spiritistic champion, championed such
seance practices as levitation, spirit writing, and spirit
apparitions. Many of these seance activities were
exposed as fraudulent by the master magician Harry
Houdini (and more recently by ex-psychic M. Lamar
Keene). In fact, so acute and complete is the recognition
of supernatural sensitivity, communication, and spirit
manifestations that several of our leading universities
have set up special divisions for the study of "extra-sen-
sory perception," or ESP. One of the most spectacular
shows connected with spiritism is known as "psychic
surgery." This is a demonic act wherein a spiritist, under
the control of his "spirit guide," supposedly performs
intricate surgical procedures without benefit of antisep-
tic, anesthesia, or surgical tools.[3] Let's look at the history
of modern spiritism.

Modern spiritism derived its impetus and inspiration
from the extraordinary "psychic" phenomena associated
with the Fox family of Hydesville (near Rochester) in
New York. The Rochester Rappings, as they have been
designated historically, began in the year 1848, when
strange rapping or knocking sounds were heard by two
young girls, Kate and Margaret Fox, the former six years
of age and the latter eight years of age. These unusual
sounds emanated from the bedroom of the two children,
and as a result of these allegedly supernatural manifestations of spirit influence, modern spiritism as a func-
tioning cult gradually evolved.

In later years the Fox sisters reputedly explained away
the rappings as "childish pranks." However, as the evidence clearly reveals today, the damage had already
been done, for out of these "manifestations" the Spiritualist Church[4] developed; and scores of mediums arose to

offer contact with departed loved ones as "bait" to attract uninformed souls toward the dark labyrinth of Spiritism.

It is interesting to note that Spiritism has made its strongest appeal to those who have suffered great losses, and after each great war, Spiritism always appears to be on the upswing—following death of a beloved husband, brother, son, etc., as a result of armed conflict.[5]

One of the great early prophets of modern-day Spiritism was Andrew Jackson Davis, a poorly educated but extremely earnest disciple of "spirit communication." In 1847 Davis published his *Principles of Nature, her divine Revelations, and a Voice to Mankind,* which is reputed to have gone through over fifty editions in the United States. To this day Davis is revered by modern spiritists as one of the great prophets of the movement.

In 1852 Spiritism was introduced into England through one Mrs. Hayden, and in Germany in 1856 there were exhibitions of so-called "spiritistic writings." Other famous "mediums" were Daniel Douglas Home, William Stainton Moses, and Leonore Piper. Chiefly through the work of these people, the famous British scientist Sir William Crooks accepted Spiritism as genuine. Later Sir Arthur Conan Doyle, along with numerous other important personages, came to recognize Spiritism as a genuine indication of the possibility of communication with the spirit world.

As we approach the theology of spiritism we are conscious of the fact that we are dealing with a most nebulous subject; most spiritists are essentially at odds with each other on interpretations of theology, which makes a concrete analysis of their beliefs difficult, to say the least. We shall now briefly survey some general beliefs held by spiritists in common and compare them with the teachings of God's Word.

The Doctrine of God

"We believe in infinite intelligence" (*Declaration of Principles,* Washington, D.C. National Spiritualist Association, p. 20, *Spiritualist Manual,* rev. 1940). This particular statement by the spiritists as to their belief regarding God is characteristic of all pantheistic cults, which rob God of His personality and reduce Him to an impersonal force which is diffused through all creation, and which in effect makes up all phenomena existing in the universe. One may find ample documentation for this fact by pursuing the literature published by the National Spiritualist Association. In fact, the second statement in its *Declaration of Principles* reads, "We believe that the phenomena of nature, both physical and spiritual, are the expression of infinite intelligence." That such a view is pantheistic, no one acquainted with spiritist literature will deny; and pantheism, regardless of how it is stated, is a denial of the personality of God, which the Bible affirms to be the very core of Christian doctrine. In the third chapter of Exodus, when the Lord spoke to Moses, He most distinctly identified Himself as a cognizant ego by stating, "I AM THAT I AM," and He added, "Thus shalt thou say unto the children of Israel, 'I AM hath sent me unto you.' " (See also Isa. 42:8; 44:6; John 8:58; Rev. 1:8-9.) From these statements it can be seen that God the Father is a reflective Ego, a personal Being, and the God and Father of the Lord Jesus Christ, the Redeemer and Saviour of all men, but "especially of those who believe." Spiritists therefore categorically deny the doctrine of the Trinity as stated in historic Christianity, and believe instead in an impersonal god—certainly not the God of the Bible!

The Person, Nature, and Work of Jesus Christ

In their proper biblical setting, these doctrines are

emphatically contradicted by all spiritist publications, and no spiritist will ever admit that salvation comes solely through the vicarious sacrifice of Christ on Calvary. Further than this, the National Spiritualist Association teaches, "We are punished by our sins and we will be happy if we obey the laws of life" *(Declaration of Principles,* Simplified Form, p. 21. *Spiritualist Manual).*

Relative to the divine nature of the Lord Jesus Christ, Spiritists affirm that He was "a prophet" and "an advanced Medium," but in no sense was He "God manifest in the flesh" (1 Tim. 3:16) for the redemption of man.[6] Throughout the length and breadth of spiritist literature one will search in vain for any statement glorifying the Lord Jesus Christ as Saviour of the world; in fact, they ascribe to Him all things except the one thing that would rightfully entitle Him to all the rest—that He is the eternal Word of God (John 1:1), the Saviour of mankind and Judge of all creation, without whom there is no salvation (Acts 4:12). The Bible, in direct contrast to the position of spiritism, states that Christ was eternal (John 8:58), that He became flesh (John 1:14), and that He died to translate men from the power of the evil one into His eternal kingdom (Col. 1:13). The Lord Jesus Christ also said, "I am the way, the truth, and the life: no man cometh unto the Father, but by me" (John 14:6)—a statement denied most energetically by all spiritists of the past and present.

The Scriptures warn that "in the last days perilous times will come . . . men will be lovers of their own selves," that they will "bring in destructive heresies, even denying the Lord that bought them." We are commanded as faithful witnesses for Christ not only to "preach the Word" with power but to shun their evil doctrines and "earnestly contend for the faith which was once delivered unto the saints" (Jude 3). Let us never forget that he who denies the deity, atonement, and resurrection of Jesus Christ, regardless of the homage he appears to pay the Lord, is, as Paul put it, an "enemy of the cross of Christ" (Phil. 3:18), and as such the wrath of God continues to abide upon him (John 3:36).

The Doctrine of the Atonement of Christ

This cardinal doctrine of the Christian faith has been attacked most strenuously by spiritists, none of whom believe that the Lord Jesus shed His blood for the remission of their sins; in fact, atonement by blood is most abhorrent to them. In spiritism one is redeemed from the power of sin by being punished in this life, or by passing through various stages of punishment in progression in the next life, until sins are atoned for. However, for the Christian "the blood of Jesus Christ, God's Son, cleanseth us from all sin" and "without the shedding of blood there is no remission"; or as the book of Leviticus puts it, "It is the blood that maketh an atonement for the soul" (17:11).

Spiritism has been most vehement in its opposition to the historic Christian doctrine of the atonement, but lest we be deceived by its pretended reverence for Christ, we should remember the historic denials rampant in its early literature and easily discernible today in its contemporary publications. When our Lord stood before Pilate, He indicated that He had come into the world to die ("To this end was I born"). Indeed, He laid much stress upon His death and His vicarious sacrifice for sinful men, and there are numerous references to this in His statements and in practically every New Testament book. The National Spiritualist Association denies this cardinal doctrine, and, for that matter, every other cardinal doctrine of the Christian faith,[7] not to mention the authority of the Bible, which is considered by them to be just another "holy book." Little more need be said about the issue in question. It is plain for all to see that spiritists beliefs are decidedly unchristian.

The Physical Resurrection of Jesus Christ

Of all the doctrines spiritists deny, the one which seems to cause them the most difficulty and at times downright consternation is the physical resurrection of Jesus Christ. The biblical position on the resurrection of Christ is quite clear. Paul states, "But now is Christ risen from the dead" (1 Cor. 15:20), and Luke 24:39 proves conclusively that Christ was not raised a spirit and did not have a spiritual resurrection, for our risen Lord said, "Behold my hands and my feet, that it is I myself; handle me, and see; for a spirit hath not flesh and bones, as ye see me have." Directly contradicting this statement, the National Spritualist Association holds that Christ was raised from the grave in a spirit form, or to quote them, "a spirit resurrection."[8] They further state that He is now an advanced medium giving regular messages from the other world. The idea of a physical resurrection is repudiated by all spiritists, and therefore we must answer, as did Paul, "If Christ be not raised, your faith is in vain; ye are yet in your sins" (1 Cor. 15:17). Tragically so they are!

We could spend a great deal more time discussing the divergent views of spiritism, especially its view of reincarnation, which teaches that spirits who have passed on have become reincarnated in other bodies, a view shared by almost all occultists but which space precludes our discussing here. We may conclude this theological survey of spiritism by drawing attention to the fact that as far as spiritism is concerned, the gospel of the Lord Jesus Christ in its historic context has been totally rejected. The only thing spiritists have retained is a semblance of Christian terminology to which they have carefully assigned different meanings, a fact amply demonstrated by the *Spiritualist Hymnal,* which takes the classic gospel hymn "Just As I Am" and renders it this way:[9]

Just as I am, thou wilt receive,
Though dogmas I may ne'er believe,
Nor heights or holiness achieve;
O God of Love, I come, I come.

Just as I am, nor poor, nor blind,
Nor bound by chains in soul or mind,
For all of thee within I find;
O God of Love, I come, I come.

They repeat this procedure with many other gospel hymns, especially those dealing with the Trinity, such as "Holy, Holy, Holy," where the triune name is completely omitted.[10] Such action should serve to warn all who may be tempted to dabble in spiritism to beware, as it is directly opposed to the gospel of Jesus Christ and should be shunned as a deadly threat to the soul.

Probably the best resumé of what spiritism really stands for is given by the *New Schaff-Herzog Encyclopedia of Religious Knowledge* (vol. II, p. 52) which states, "They reject the doctrine of the Trinity and of the deity of Christ, and also that of the supreme authority of the Scriptures; they hold to the existence of an infinite intelligence expressed by the physical and spiritual phenomena of nature, a correct understanding of which and a following of which in life constitute the true religion; the continued conscious existence of the spirit after death is a postulate, and with this goes belief in progress as the universal law of nature."

A careful perusal of contemporary spiritist literature

will confirm the truth of this condensed but succinct statement.

Now that we have explored some of the aberrant beliefs of occultists (as represented by spiritism), we need to address the question of *why* people are attracted to occultic practices, beliefs, and groups.

There are many reasons people turn to the world of darkness, some of which we will review here. Most of the attraction of the occult stems from problems individuals have with relating to others, the world around them, and, most importantly, God. Some causes are unique to our present electronic age and some are as old as mankind itself.

Causes unique to our society usually relate to what people see as social alienation. People are not satisfied with electronic impersonalization. They don't want to be a twelve-digit account number relating to a computer. They rebel against the rigid authority of the scientific/technological hierarchy which appears to reign supreme in developed countries today. Instead, they turn to the allure of personal knowledge and personal power offered enticingly by the occult. "Shorted out" by electronic wizardry and cold calculations, people gravitate towards the irrational and exciting.

Christians and non-Christians alike seem to believe that there is an irreconcilable dichotomy between reason and faith, between logic and belief. Dissatisfied with mathematical "reason," people turn to "faith and belief" in magic, the supernatural, and psychic phenomena, seemingly unaware of the fact that the supernatural Creator of the universe, our Lord Jehovah, is the author of all truth, logic, and reason, and that faith and belief in Him is the most reasonable option available to all of mankind.

Many of the causes of occultic involvement have

always been common to non-Christians. People have always preferred "black and white" distinctions. They are uncomfortable with vague generalizations, loose categories, and relativistic standards. Unfortunately, today's Christian Church has often succumbed to the temptation to blur the lines of distinction between the faithful and the pagan, the believers and the nonbelievers. Many people are dissatisfied with this hypocrisy and often turn completely the other direction to open Satan worship as a declaration of the important religious distinctions dishonestly obscured.

People have always been interested in power, often confusing the possession thereof with divine favor. Just because one can bend spoons "psychically" does not mean that one possesses the blessings and power of God.

People have always been curious about the future. In fact, more occultic practices and devices relate to revealing and understanding the future than all other occultic practices and devices combined. The promise of being able to see the future is one of the strongest attractions of the world of the occult. However, the God of the Bible reminds us that no man or demon can declare the future: "Who hath declared from the beginning, that we may know? and beforetime, that we may say, He is righteous? yea, there is none that sheweth, yea, there is none that declareth, yea, there is none that heareth your words" (Isa. 41:26). In fact, only the all-knowing (omniscient) God of the Bible can declare the future, saying, "I have declared the former things from the beginning; and they went forth out of my mouth, and I shewed them; I did them suddenly, and they came to pass . . . . I have even from the beginning declared it to thee; before it came to pass I shewed it thee: lest thou shouldest say, Mine idol hath done them, and my graven image, and my molten image, hath commanded them" (Isa. 48:3,5).

Finally, people have always been searching for purpose, security, and personal relationships. This need for acceptance and love is exploited by occultism (and, indeed, by the cults too). Those interested in the occult are promised attention, security, purpose, love. Not until they are caught in the dark web do they discover that the price for such things is eternal separation from the God who is the only one ultimately able to satisfy those needs.

There are, then, many attractions in the world of the occult, many causes of the occultic manifestation we see today. However, all of these attractions and causes are meaningless since they deny the truth, authority, and love of the Lord of the universe and His Son, Jesus Christ.

The attitude which the Bible as a whole takes toward the practice of establishing "contact" with the spirit world is very well known.

Today throughout the world, even as it was in the days of ancient occultism, men still dabble in a sphere so dangerous to the soul that God commanded death under the Mosaic Law for spiritistic mediums convicted of necromancy (Lev. 20:27). Man's ancient and unholy desire to explore the realms of God's domain is very much alive, and today zealous spiritists are actively proselytizing converts among any and all who will listen.

The true Christian attitude toward spiritism must be one of hostility, theologically speaking, tempered with the desire to win the cultist to a saving faith in the Lord Jesus Christ. The Bible irrevocably warns against tampering with the realms of existence beyond human comprehension, and, as in the case of Saul and Samuel's spirit (1 Sam. 28:14), the results usually evoke divine judgment of a severe nature. Therefore, let us beware of such forbidden dangers.

Another common danger which spiritism introduces is that of demon possession, since the Scriptures quite definitely reveal that demon power and influence is present in most genuine manifestations of spiritistic phenomena. No Christian therefore should ever allow himself to be exposed to demon influence if it possibly can be avoided, for their presence is direct testimony to Satan's part in the unholy seance; no intelligent Christian should be found in attendance in such forbidden satanic rites. However, the Scriptures also teach that no believer can be indwelt by demons or possessed by demons, since we are the "temple of God" and "God's Spirit dwells in you" (1 Cor. 3:16). "Greater is he that is in you, than he that is in the world" (1 John 4:4). But other dangers are still involved in such contacts, and they should be shunned at all costs.

It is imperative that Christians understand spiritism and its contemporary resurgence in the light of biblical prophecy. Prophecy teaches us that "the doctrines of demons" will multiply in "the last times," and that this is sound evidence indeed that the coming of our Lord draws nigh. Let those who truly "love His appearing" be prepared for the rise of false cults and doctrines, that we may warn the "other sheep" and the Lord's flock of those "having a form of godliness but denying the power thereof" (2 Tim. 3:5).

NOTES

1. We are using spiritism as generally representative of occultic practices and groups.

2. H. Jacquet, Jr., ed., *The 1978 Yearbook of American and Canadian Churches* (Nashville: Abingdon Press, 1978).

3. See Johanna Michaelsen's *The Beautiful Side of Evil* (Eugene, OR: Harvest House Publishers, 1982).

4. *Spiritualist* and its derivatives are misnomers. Those participating in and advocating such demonic activities as we discuss here are anything but spiritual. *Spiritist* and its derivatives correctly identify the demonic source.

5. See Earl E. Cairns, *Christianity Through the Centuries,* rev. ed. (Grand Rapids: Zondervan Publishing House, 1981), p. 423.

6. See *The Two Worlds,* March 10, 1956, p. 8.

7. *The Two Worlds,* p. 8.

8. *The Natural Spiritualist,* April, 1956, p. 4.

9. The *Spiritualist Hymnal,* p. 43.

10. Ibid., p. 49.

six
The New Cults

Never in the history of Christianity has there been such a public awareness of the dangerous world of the cults as there is now, among Christians and non-Christians alike. Cults have been with us since the Church began almost two thousand years ago and Jesus told His disciples that false Christs and false prophets or teachers would be one of the signs of the end of the world as we know it. However, there is a new "flavor" to the cults springing up around us throughout the United States today.

The cults of the New Testament Church were loosely organized, usually borrowed from the mystery religions around them, and boldly exposed and refuted by the New Testament writers. The cults of the early post-New Testament Church were more organized, developed their aberrant theologies more intricately, but were still soundly refuted and unanimously condemned by the leaders of the early Church.

The traditional cults (largely represented by the cults discussed in the preceding chapters of this book), with which the more modern Church has had to contend, borrowed some from previous cults and introduced some novel features of their own. Almost all of the traditional cults have the same kinds of nonbiblical doctrines as were held by the cults condemned in the early centuries of the Church. Almost all of the traditional cults claim to be the restoration of the true, original, and biblical Christianity which disappeared (supposedly) sometime in the early centuries of the Church. However, the traditional cults emphasize for the first time the absolute leadership of one (or at the most a select few) "charismatic" leaders. The role of cult leader has become the single most important ingredient in the traditional cults' systems. We have seen in this book how Charles Taze Russell, Joseph Smith, Jr., Mary Baker Eddy and Charles and Myrtle Fillmore were the creating and inspiring powers behind the growth of their respective cults.

For the first time, too, the Church's response has not been unanimous. This is almost entirely due to the fragmented and schismatic nature of nineteenth- and twentieth-century Christianity. There is no "consensus of the Church" which reflects the convictions and support of all of the major leaders of the Christian Church. The great doctrines of our faith, so clearly and forcefully presented in the Scriptures, are not held universally by all parts and members of the Church. With liberals who doubt the deity of Christ in the midst of the Church, how can the Church condemn those cultists who deny His deity? Also, to a very small extent this lack of unanimous condemnation has been caused by the sophisticated terminology and doctrinal twisting done by the cults.

The new cults brought new twists to the cult scene beginning in the early 1960s and continuing almost unabated through today, despite the horrible massacre of Jonestown and the criminal convictions of more than one new cult leader (such as the convictions of several high-ranking leaders, including cult founder L. Ron Hubbard's wife, of the Scientology cult). Most of the new cults (among them are the Family of Love, once known as the Children of God; the Unification Church; the Hare Krishnas, officially known as the International Society for Krishna Consciousness; est, which stands for Erhard Seminars Training; the "Church" of Scientology; and TM, which stands for Transcendental Meditation) do not claim to be the restoration of biblical Christianity but instead claim to have a new and better revelation than that given in the Bible by Jesus Christ. Thus we see Family of Love founder, "Moses" David Berg, claiming to have a better revelation than Jesus brought, and that his own writings are superior to the Bible; the Unification Church's Rev. Sun Myung Moon claiming to be the "Lord of the Second Advent," completing what Jesus Christ only began; the Hare Krishnas claiming that Krishna *created* Jesus Christ; est's Werner Erhard claiming that we do not need the Bible but only need to realize that we are our own gods (Jesus Christ knew this but was too "selfish" to let us in on the secret); Scientology's L. Ron Hubbard claiming to be the most spiritually advanced and pure being who has ever existed on this earth; and TM founder Maharishi Mahesh Yogi claiming that with his meditation one doesn't need the Bible at all.

The new cults are also novel in that they have a special orientation and appeal to young people, particularly college students. The new cults promote their own carefully controlled "education," often passing out degrees and ordinations to their most promising "students." Most of the new cults incorporate some form of eastern or Hindu thought in their complex and evolving theologies. And many of the new cults are deeply involved in the very practices we discussed in the last chapters, the occultic/psychic phenomena which is in the domain of Satan himself. So we see that there are some unique aspects to the rise of what we shall term here the *new cults.* They are, in a very real sense, the fulfillment of Jesus' warning in Matthew 24 that in the very last days false Christs, false prophets, and false teachers would arise, deceiving many and even seeking to deceive Christians.

Following are some of the most important characteristics of the new cults, which are a very real threat to the Christian Church today. Over twenty-five million people around the world are involved to some extent in the new cults. Although the figure is much smaller in the United States, their number cannot be discounted and their proselytizing zeal is a threat to be countered by the gospel.[1]

1. The new cults are usually started by strong and dynamic leaders who are in complete control of their followers. This power is said to be supernatural, divine in origin, and to be a proof of their "calling" by God.

2. The new cults possess and promote revelation that usually replaces or supercedes the Bible (or sometimes, as in the case of The Way International, radically and "divinely" reinterpret the Bible).

3. The new cults have rigid and demanding standards for membership and will accept and retain only those members who give of themselves completely and without reservation. Those who deviate in the least from the cult's regulations are severely disciplined, ostracized if necessary and, if they don't repent, are excommuni-

cated with little hope of ever being accepted again.

4. The new cults are actively evangelistic or mission-ary minded in the sense that their recruitment program is a top priority and cult growth is seen as a sign of divine favor on the group. Some cults even instill the idea that a measure of one's loyalty to the group is demonstrated by his ability to bring new members into the fold.

5. Most new cult leaders are not professional or pub-licly recognized clergymen. They are, for the most part, self-appointed spokesmen for God. They seldom pos-sess more than a passing acquaintance with Bible col-lege or seminary and even less familiarity with biblical theology.

6. The new cults possess a body of doctrine which is in a constant state of flux. This shifting and development is caused partly by the recent origins of the cults. They just haven't had enough time to systematize and inte-grate their whole theology. However, each member is expected to learn this shifting system and will be ostra-cized immediately if he deviates from it. This helps pre-serve the need for a living leader and spokesman for God, who can interpret God's latest "truth." This also causes the members to depend on the leaders every minute—they never know when something will be changed.

7. The new cults also claim exclusive possession of religious and spiritual truth. While they may pay lip ser-vice to the idea of "truth along many paths" (a favorite Hindu idea), they each know within the group that they exclusively have God's ultimate and complete revelation.

8. The new cults take most of the standard terms of Christianity and the Bible and redefine them, giving them an in-group meaning that is hidden from outsid-ers. Thus the Hare Krishnas can say that "Jesus loves Krishna" but mean that Jesus is a creation of Lord

Krishna! The Moonies can say they believe in the "Messiah" but mean Moon instead of Jesus Christ!

There are literally thousands of cults throughout the United States. It would be impossible in a survey of this size to review all of the doctrines of even the top twenty new cults.[2] However, we hope that the summaries of the teachings of the five new cults presented below will aid the reader in identifying and refuting biblically the false claims of the new cults.

Hare Krishnas

Krishna (sometimes spelled *Krsna*) is the supreme personal God of ISKCON:

"... Lord Sri Krsna is the original Personality of Godhead Himself" (*Srimad Bhagavatam* 1:3:28).

Krsna, Who is known as Govinda, is the Supreme Godhead. He has no eternal, blissful spiritual body" (*Brahma Samhita* 5:1).

Jesus Christ is only the created Son of Lord Krishna (see Siddha Swarup Ananda Goswami, *Jesus Loves Krsna*, p. 26).

Sin and Salvation to the Hare Krishnas is related to their belief in reincarnation and karmic retribution for bad deeds. One is cleansed of his sin only by personal *yoga*, a Hindu word meaning an exercise (spiritual, mental, or physical) designated to rid one of accumulated karma and elevate one towards ultimate freedom from sin and unfettered worship of Krishna. Jesus Christ is *not* the only means of salvation:

All these performers who know the meaning
of sacrifice become cleansed of sinful reactions

(Prabhupada, *Bhagavad-Gita As It Is,* 4:30).

. . . God sent Jesus to be the spiritual master of particular people in a particular time and place . . . . He did not claim (as others claim today) that He was the only Representative or Agent of the Supreme Person ever to walk the earth in the past or future (ibid., p. 44).

TM (Transcendental Meditation)

God to founder Maharishi Mahesh Yogi is ultimately pantheistic and impersonal. Maharishi worships the God/gods of classical Hinduism in western, secular terminology:

> Everything is Brahman (to) the performer who is established in Cosmic Consciousness . . . . Brahman is the state of Cosmic Consciousness . . . . Brahman, which is an all pervading mass of bliss, does not exhibit any quality of bliss (Maharishi Mahesh Yogi, *On the Bhagavad-Gita,* pp. 291,364,440-441).

Jesus Christ to Maharishi Mahesh Yogi never suffered and died for our sins and was, as are all people, ultimately one with Brahman, the impersonal Cosmic Consciousness.

> I don't think Christ ever suffered or Christ could suffer . . . it is a pity that Christ is talked of in terms of suffering . . . those who count upon the suffering [for salvation, have] a wrong interpretation of the life of Christ and the message of Christ. It is wrong (Maharishi Mahesh Yogi, *Meditations of Maharishi,* p. 124).

Sin and Salvation according to TM is similar to that of the Hare Krishnas, both cults deriving their teachings from classical Hinduism. TM teaches that one's sins can be atoned for only by one's *own* actions. Salvation is self-made and one's ultimate reward is to lose his individuality and merge into the eternal bliss of Brahman:

> It is because the Self is joined in Union with Brahman that a man enjoys eternal happiness (Maharishi Mahesh Yogi, *On the Bhagavad-Gita,* p. 365).
>
> Having gained the state of Brahman, a man has risen to the ultimate Reality of existence. In this state of enlightenment he has accomplished eternal liberation (Maharishi Mahesh Yogi, *On the Bhagavad-Gita,* p. 247).
>
> The key to fulfillment of every religion is found in the regular practice of transcendental deep meditation (ibid., p. 291).

The Unification Church

God to founder Sun Myung Moon is an inconsistent combination of Hindu and Buddhist dualism and Christian monotheism. He is not the God of the Bible:

> . . . God's essential positivity and essential negativity are the attributes of His essential character and essential form . . . . Here we call the positivity and negativity of God "masculinity" and "femininity," respectively (Sun Myung Moon, *Divine Principle,* p. 24).
>
> We act like we do because God acts that way. That's the way God is! That's the way we are. We are like God, and God is like us" (Sun Myung Moon, *The New Future of Christianity,* p. 28).

Jesus Christ to the Moonies is not uniquely God the Son. He is God only as others may be or become one with God:

> The Principle does not deny the attitude of faith held by many Christians that Jesus is God, since it is true that a [any] perfected man is one body with God (*Divine Principle,* p. 209).
>
> Jesus, on earth, was a man no different from us except for the fact that he was without original sin (ibid., p. 212).

Sin and Salvation in Unification theology involves two "falls": one spiritual and one physical. Jesus Christ only obtained our spiritual redemption. It remains for the "Lord of the Second Advent" (Moon) to redeem us physically:

> If Jesus had not been crucified, what would have happened? He would have accomplished the providence of salvation both spiritually and physically (ibid., p. 147).
>
> God will give you your own salvation. When you become God's champion for world salvation, our own salvation is guaranteed (Sun Myung Moon, *New Hope,* p. 49).

The Way International

God to The Way International is only the Father (sometimes called the Holy Spirit) and *Jesus Christ* is *not* God. This is taught by the cult's founder, Victor Paul Wierwille:

The doctrine of the trinity states that the Father

is God, the Son is God, the Holy Spirit is God and together, not exclusively, they form one God. The trinity is co-eternal, without beginning and end, and co-equal. That defines the doctrine of the trinity, and this I do not believe the Bible teaches .... I am saying that Jesus Christ is not God ... (Victor Paul Wierwille, *Jesus Christ is Not God*, p. 5).

Sin and Salvation in the theology of The Way International is a complicated system wherein one regains his "spirit" (which ceased to exist at the fall) by faith in Jesus Christ (who is *not* God) and repentance of one's sin. But rather than adhering to the biblical concept of personal responsibility for sin, from this point according to The Way the Christian cannot sin in his "spirit":

When the natural man is born again, in what part of his being does he not commit sin? In his body and soul he still commits sin; but in that seed of God which is incorruptible [the spirit], he does not commit sin (Victor Paul Wierwille, *Power for Abundant Living*, p. 292).

Scientology

Founder L. Ron Hubbard, a former science fiction writer, teaches a concept of *God* which also seems almost like science fiction. God to Hubbard and Scientologists cannot be defined, but He certainly is more than one (polytheistic):

There are gods above all other gods, and gods beyond the gods of the universe ... (L. Ron Hubbard, *Scientology 8-8008*, p. 73).

Jesus Christ to the Scientologists was not the Supreme God Incarnate, the unique Son of God. Instead, he was only moderately advanced in his own spiritual odyssey:

> Neither Lord Buddha nor Jesus Christ were OT's [Operating Thetans, a high state of spiritual perfection] according to the evidence. They were just a shade above clear (L. Ron Hubbard, *Certainty* magazine, vol. 5, no. 10).

There is no need of *salvation* in the Scientologist's system since there is no real *sin*—one only need work through Scientology's system, realizing his own divinity, to achieve "salvation":

> Man is basically god but he could not attain expression of this until now. Nobody but the individual could die for his own sins—to arrange things otherwise was to keep man in chains (L. Ron Hubbard, *The Volunteer Minister's Handbook,* p. 349).
>
> Scientology is a religious philosophy with spiritual guidance procedures enabling an individual to attain Total Spiritual Freedom (L. Ron Hubbard, *Axioms and Logics,* inside front cover).

These five new cults are representative of the false doctrines of the new cults. I could go on for literally volumes listing and discussing the teachings of the new cults. However, this small introduction to the realm of the new cults should serve as a warning to the non-Christian to beware of the sugared spiritual poison offered so temptingly by the new cults in America today.

This should also serve as a warning to Christians to take up the standard of truth, "put on the whole armor of God" (Eph. 6), and "defend the faith" (see 1 Pet. 3:15) of our Lord and Saviour, Jesus Christ.

NOTES

1. For further information on the characteristics of the new cults, see my book *The New Cults* (Ventura, CA: Vision House, 1980), pp. 11-35.

2. For further information, see *The New Cults* and *Walter Martin's Cults Reference Bible* (Ventura, CA: Vision House, 1981).

seven

Meeting the Challenge of the Cults

The universal cry in our area, which appears to be stirring the sleeping giant of orthodoxy, is: "Where did the cults come from? What can be done to combat them effectively?"

As has been shown amply, the major cults out-propagandize and outgive evangelical Christianity in the support of their beliefs, and they threaten in no small way to endanger every mission field on the globe, which until recently was largely free from concentrated cult activities. Unfortunately, some Christians take the attitude of a gentleman I spoke with thirty-five years ago, who enjoyed the distinction of being one of the leading publishers of Christian books in the United States.

I approached this distinguished gentleman at the time, hoping he would accept and publish a manuscript

I had written which was an exposé of Jehovah's Witnesses. The coauthor and I offered the manuscript for publication at no profit to ourselves, and we even offered to let the publisher remove our names from the book, as we were then unknown in the writing field.

Mr. X, as we shall call him, thoroughly read the manuscript which we left with him. When we returned the next day he had nothing but good things to say about it.

"The Christian public needs books like this," he said emphatically. "I have never seen a more thorough job of documentation than you have done on this subject—it should be a best-seller in its field. I personally wish every Christian who meets a Jehovah's Witness could have a copy of this. I think you have done a fine job and I wish you success."

Upon hearing such lavish praise as this we fully expected to see the book printed in a very short time, but we were doomed to quick disappointment, for we did not then know that a glib tongue often camouflages a quaking heart.

Thinking that at last we could speak of publication, we pressed Mr. X for details and received the following comment: "Please do not misunderstand me, gentlemen. Though I like the book I cannot publish it. You see, I believe that we ought to let the Lord rebuke the devil, and these cults are devilish, so I take the position of the Archangel Michael when he contended with the devil (Jude 9) and I just say, 'The Lord rebuke thee,' for I have no desire to be involved with Jehovah's Witnesses."

We explained to Mr. X that there was no legal risk in printing the book, as three lawyers had already passed favorably on its contents, and that he would make a reasonable profit on it because it was the only book written on the subject and was therefore a primary source for pastors and interested laymen. However, all our protestations were to no avail. Mr. X continued in his "let alone" theory despite Jude 3 and our pointing out to him that his use of Jude 9 was completely at variance with the contextual meaning.

Finally, in desperation, we attempted to find out if what we had suspected all along was true, and we pointedly asked Mr. X the following question:

"Are you afraid to print this book because you fear the reprisals of the Watchtower?"

Mr. X colored noticeably, and raising his voice stammered, "I—I do not wish to become involved in litigation with any organization as big as the Watchtower, so I say again regarding the cults, 'The Lord rebuke thee,' and that is my decision."

We left Mr. X with heaviness in our hearts, but as we passed out of his office we saw a sign over the door which added that touch of humor so often needed in dark situations. The sign read in large bold type: "If God is your partner, make your plans big."

Here was a man who ignored the commands of Scripture without blinking, and yet expressed as his motto complete trust in the promises of God. This was indeed both humorous and paradoxical, but it gave us an unforgettable glimpse of a type of thinking all too prevalent in our day. Pious temerity, we believe, has no place on the battlefield of the heavenlies (see Eph. 6:12).

FACING THE CULTS

I believe there is a definite solution to the problem of cults, and I think that this solution can be aided by any and all Christians willing to cooperate. Here are the facts which can greatly facilitate grasping the significance of cult problems.

1. The cults came from dissatisfied souls who, because they could not understand biblical Christianity

(or having understood it, rejected it) preferred instead the religious opinions of kindred souls.

2. The cults grew to their present proportions because persons of similar persuasions sided with the "underdog," and the Christian Church as a whole failed to meet the challenge in a positive and unified way.

3. The challenge of cultism can be met only with a systematic program dedicated to a thorough education of all Christians, clergy and laity, in the basic tenets, approaches, and propaganda activities of the major non-Christian cults.

Only recently have Christians and churches in the United States taken seriously the challenge of the cults and responded with a defense of the true gospel. Even so, this response has been sporadic, disorganized, uninformed, and often too late for many who permanently are caught in the web of deception spun by the cults of our day. I have been warning against the false teachings of the cults and sharing the good news with cultists for over thirty-five years and founded my own Christian Research Institute twenty-three years ago, and still Christians complacently sit back and wait for "those sincere and sweet people" to "come to their senses." What kind of Christian love is it that will sit idly by while thousands of people unwittingly follow a lie? No Christian can ignore the pleas of those caught in the cults without facing the judgment of Jesus Christ. How often I have heard an ex-cultist say, "Nobody ever talked to me like you did. I didn't know there was something better. Thank you and thank the Lord!"

I founded and am the director of an interdenominational research organization, the Christian Research Institute, which is the first contemporary counter-cult organization, the model after which other groups, successfully waging the "battle," patterned themselves. The

Institute's purpose is to supply primary data on all the cults, and non-Christian missionary activities, both here and abroad. It is the function of this Institute to index the major cults and to supply resumés of their origin, history, and doctrines, with bibliographical material aimed at specifically evangelizing and refuting their respective teachings.

To Christian colleges and seminaries CRI has proven to be most valuable because it fills a great need. Though strong counter-cult curricula are offered in *some* colleges and seminaries, not nearly enough are offered in general, since confusion on what cultists believe and a general inability to cope with them effectively in the pastorate is unfortunately much in evidence. To refute cultism, *the Christian public must know what cultists believe and why they believe it.* But more important, Christians must know *why they believe orthodox theology,* since it is mainly through the contrast of sound doctrine with heresy that error is exposed and refuted.

The Christian Church today must face the fact that unless unified action is taken against the tremendous upsurge of cultism in both the United States and numerous foreign mission fields, the Church in this decade will be fighting for its apologetic life against an enemy whose growth is directly proportional to the Church's failure to educate its members to the insidious doctrines of the cults. God grant that many will see this grave danger and rise up to the defense of the gospel.

There are many people today who feel that "preaching the Word" is a "positive" message, and that "contending for the faith" is a "negative" approach. But such is not the teaching of the Scriptures.

The Apostle Paul, who wrote a great part of the New Testament, devoted a vast amount of space to "sound doctrine," always comparing it with the false teachings of others, whom he termed "beasts" and against whom he frequently "wrestled." The Pauline Epistles abound in attacks upon false philosophies (see Romans vs. Pharisees, Galatians vs. Judaizers, Ephesians vs. general error, Philippians and Colossians vs. Gnosticism, etc.).

The Apostle Peter never ceased to warn of those "who privily shall bring in damnable heresies, even denying the Lord that bought them" (2 Pet. 2:1), and Jude describes them as "raging waves of the sea, foaming out their own shame; wandering stars, to whom is reserved the blackness of darkness forever" (Jude 13).

Far from being a "negative approach," the task of apologetics is a vitally positive ministry, and one that was actively followed by the prophets, Christ, Paul, Peter, John, Jude, and many others. The Christian today who does not recognize this fact, or worse, refuses to engage in apologetics when he realizes its importance, is in direct disobedience to the revealed will of God and cannot forever escape judgment of a severe nature.

Let us join our forces to resist the onslaught of corrupt doctrines so evident in cultism. And as we lift our hearts in faith and our lives by obedience to the divine command, we shall become aware that the "sleeping giant" of orthodoxy no longer slumbers, but that the Church has at last grasped "the sword of the Spirit," and is even now coming "to the help of the Lord against the mighty" (Judg. 5:23).

Appendix
Armstrong/Worldwide Church of God

The rise of the Worldwide Church of God is one of the truly phenomenal stories in the growth of American cultism. Beginning in 1934 under the direction of its founder, Herbert W. Armstrong, it continues today (nearly fifty years later) to be the most vocal of all indigenous American cult systems.

Though Herbert Armstrong is now an octogenarian, he still has a major voice in the policies and teachings of the church he founded. However, the real power in what has been termed "the Armstrong empire" was his dynamic, personable, and highly persuasive successor in back of the microphone and in front of the TV cameras, Garner Ted Armstrong. I think it may be said without contradiction that Garner Ted was a master of communications and knew how to utilize the media advantageously in the spreading of his religion.

In January of 1972 a rift developed between Herbert Armstrong and his son, Garner Ted, who was exiled for four months by the senior Armstrong. Herbert said his son was "in the bonds of Satan." After "heartfelt repentance," Garner Ted was restored to church fellowship and returned as the voice of the "World Tomorrow" broadcast. His apparent sins were never made public, but in 1974 six prominent church ministers resigned from the Worldwide Church of God, naming as griefs alleged sexual misconduct by Garner Ted over a period of years, squandered church monies and disputed doctrines. This action proved to be prophetic, for in 1978 Garner Ted was excommunicated by his father for some of these same reasons. Garner Ted has established the Church of God, International, in Tyler, Texas, in retaliation. He has a mailing list of some five thousand names and a reported daily church income of $2,000.

Later in 1978 a handful of Worldwide Church of God members, working with an attorney, presented the attorney general of the State of California with a legal brief. The brief was prepared because the members had become concerned over the rapid liquidation of church properties after the younger Armstrong's excommunication. A civil suit was prepared naming the disgruntled members and the people of the State of California as plaintiffs. The defendants were Herbert Armstrong, Stanley R. Rader, the Worldwide Church of God, Inc., Ambassador College, Inc., and others. The charges centered on financial matters, especially the alleged siphoning off of millions of church dollars for personal use by Mr. Armstrong and Rader. The suit called for an accounting of all funds and financial transactions of the defendants, not for monetary damages to the plaintiffs. The church was placed in receivership, in effect giving all control of church financial matters to a neutral party.

From his home in Tucson, Arizona, Mr. Armstrong effected a confusing shake-up of church leadership. First, he named C. Wayne Cole as executive director of the church, replacing Rader. Only hours later Cole was replaced by C. Roderick Meredith, a conservative and supporter of Rader. Cole and three other church leaders were then excommunicated. Meanwhile, the receiver placed over the Worldwide Church of God by the courts quit, claiming non-cooperation by church leaders. The receivership was lifted in favor of an independent audit. Rader first agreed to the audit, then attacked it, claiming all attempts to audit church financial records as a conspiracy to violate the church's civil rights. A second receivership was placed on the church, but a loophole allowed the church to post a $1 million bond to stay the order. The issue, says Rader, is over the government's attempted control of internal church affairs. Recent California legislative activity (1980) has seriously circumscribed the California attorney general's powers regarding investigation and prosecution of the Worldwide Church of God and other nonprofit religious organizations.

Of all the cultic structures, the Worldwide Church of God sponsors more radio broadcasts and television programs on more stations than any other cultic group in the world, and in fact more than its five top competitors combined![1] Herbert W. Armstrong has made it a career to become a senior statesman of diplomacy for his church, and visits the various leaders of established and emerging nations, attracting their attention by his expensive gifts and direct-aid programs in areas where the individual country may be in need.

An example of Mr. Armstrong's diplomacy is his high standing with the Israeli government, for whom he has sponsored archeological digs, not the least of which are his much-publicized excavations around and underneath the site of the second temple in Jerusalem.

The Armstrong religion is strong in England, throughout the United Kingdom, and on the European continent, as well as in the United States. It should be noted that Radio Luxembourg and other stations beam Mr. Armstrong's material all over Europe and behind the Iron Curtain, so the work of the church is not strange to them.

One of the greatest mistakes the Christian Church has made in relation to Mr. Armstrong is that it has not recognized his mastery of the world of communications and the persuasiveness of his eclectic theology.

Herbert Armstrong was influenced in his early days by the Seventh-Day Adventists denomination and also by the writings of Charles Russell, founder of the Watchtower Bible and Tract Society, better know today as Jehovah's Witnesses. Though Mr. Armstrong vigorously denies any influence from outside sources relative to his doctrines, one need only listen to him for a period of one or two months and the roots of his theological thought emerge quite clearly.

One of the reasons it is so difficult to pin Mr. Armstrong's errors down is that he sounds like Billy Graham when he says "Jesus is God" one week; the next week like Mormonism, "You can become divine"; the next week like the original Jehovah's Witnesses organization; the next week like the Seventh-Day Adventists; and finally, like the Anglo-Israel or British-Israel cult.

From the Mormons he can say that, yes, Jesus is God, but only in the sense that *we too* may become part of the "god family," just as Jesus is. From Seventh-Day Adventism he has borrowed the observance of the seventh-day Sabbath, abstinence from unclean foods (pork, lobster, crab, etc.), and certain methods of prophetic interpretation. From the Dawn Bible Students he lifted the doctrine that Charles Russell taught, namely, that no one is now born again until the resurrection, Jesus Christ being the sole exception. He also borrowed from the Jehovah's Witnesses the teaching that Satan and all unregenerate men will be annihilated, and that man remains unconscious in the grave until the resurrection. Mr. Armstrong also adopts the Jehovah's Witnesses' view of the resurrection of Jesus Christ, and declares that Christ was raised from the dead as a spirit, not as an immortal man with a physical form of flesh and bone. From Anglo-Israelism Armstrong borrowed the teaching that Great Britain and the United States are the ten lost tribes of Israel, which can only be described as a prophetic hallucination discounted by all great scholars of the Hebrew language, of archeology, and of history as without foundation.

It depends, then, on what week you listen to Mr. Armstrong as to what his theological position will be, for he is indeed the cultic chameleon of the airwaves, changing color with the exposition of each borrowed doctrine and then neatly homogenizing all of the parts into a simplistic view of God, the world, and the Bible. The Christian gospel itself is carefully redefined and made palatable to the minds of men unlearned in Mr. Armstrong's pronouncements as they refer to the historic teachings of the Word of God.

As we shall see when we analyze Mr. Armstrong's theology, it all rests upon his claim that the Worldwide Church of God is the only church preaching the same gospel the Lord Jesus Christ preached and that the apostles preached. On this point Mr. Armstrong is adamant:

> I'm going to give you the frank and straight

answer. You have a right to know all about this great work of God, and about me. First, let me say—this may sound incredible, but it's true— *Jesus Christ foretold this very work—it is, itself, the fulfillment of his prophecy* (Matthew 24:14 and Mark 13:10).

Astounding as it may seem, there is no other work on earth proclaiming to the whole world *this very same gospel* that Jesus taught and proclaimed!

And *listen again!* Read this twice! Realize this, incredible though it may seem—*no other work on earth is proclaiming this true Gospel of Christ to the whole world* as Jesus foretold in Matthew 24:14 and Mark 13:10! This is the most important activity on earth today![2]

The prophecies bring this Church into concrete focus in the 12th chapter of Revelation. There she is shown spiritually, in the glory and splendor of the Spirit of God, but visibly in the world as a persecuted, Commandment-keeping Church *driven into the wilderness,* for 1,260 years, thru the middle ages!

In New Testament prophecy *two churches* are described.

One, the great and powerful and universal church, a *part* of the world, actually ruling in its politics over many nations, and united with the "Holy Roman Empire," brought to a concrete focus in Revelation 17.

. . . She is a *mother* Church! Her daughters are also *churches* who have come out of her, even in protest, calling themselves Protestant— but they are fundamentally of her family in pagan doctrines and practices! They, too, make themselves a *part of* this world, taking active part in its politics—the very act which made a "whore" out of their *Mother!*

The entire apostate family—Mother, and more than 500 daughter denominations, all divided against each other and in *confusion* of doctrines, yet all united in the chief pagan doctrines and festivals—has a family *name!* They call themselves "Christian," but God calls them something else!—"*Mystery, Babylon the Great!*"

But the true Church of God is pictured in prophecy as the "*Little* Flock!" . . . It has kept God's festivals . . . .

That Church always has existed, and it exists today![3]

Yet, is there *anything* so shocking—so hard to believe—as this flat Biblical statement that the whole world is religiously deceived?

Thirty-seven years ago *I* simply couldn't believe it—until I found it *proved!* And even then, my head was swimming: I found myself all mixed up. To see with my own eyes in the Bible precisely the *opposite* of what I had been taught from boyhood in Sunday School: well, this was pretty hard to take! Yet, there it was, in plain type before my eyes!

If *this* were the year 30 A.D. and you took a trip to Jerusalem, and there speaking to a throng around Him you should see an ordinary looking young man about the age of 33 teaching the same things you hear me and Garner Ted Armstrong say over the radio today, it would have been just as astonishing to you then as it is today—and as it was to those who heard Him then . . . . You would have been truly *astonished!* His doctrine was so different! And He spoke dogmatically with assurance; with power and *authority* . . . . But He had foretold apostasy. He had foretold "wolves" coming in "sheep's clothing" to *deceive* the world. He had said they would *enter* in professing to come in *His name*—claiming to be *Christian*—yet deceiving the whole world. *That happened!*

For two 19-year time cycles the original apostles did proclaim His *Gospel*—the Gospel of the Kingdom of God. But in 69 A.D. they fled. In 70 A.D. came the military siege against Jerusalem. The ministers of Satan (II Cor. 11:13-15) had wormed their way in, had gained such power that by persecution and political influence they were able to brand the *true* people of God as heretics, and prevent further organized proclaiming of the same Gospel Christ brought from God. For 18½ centuries that Gospel was not preached. The world was deceived into accepting a *false* gospel. Today Christ has raised up *His Work* and once again allotted two 19-year time cycles for proclaiming His *same Gospel,* preparatory to *His Second Coming* . . . . *The World Tomorrow* and *The Plain Truth* are *Christ's instruments* which He is powerfully using. Yes, His message is shocking today. Once again it is the voice in the wilderness of religious confusion![4]

"No man ever spoke like this man," reported their officers to the Pharisees regarding Jesus.

The multitudes "were astonished at His doctrine."

Today the same *living Christ,* through *The World Tomorrow* broadcast, *The Plain Truth* magazine, and *this Work,* proclaims in mighty power *around the world* His *same Gospel—the same* Gospel preached by Peter, Paul, and the original Apostles.[5]

Mr. Armstrong's view of his role, and that of the Worldwide Church of God, parallels the claim of all non-Christian cultic leaders, namely, that they are the messengers of God uniquely set apart to either "restore" or to "correctly reinterpret" the Christian message. Charles Russell, founder of Jehovah's Witnesses, maintained that ignorance of his writings could send one into spiritual darkness within two years. Mary Baker Eddy maintained that her discovery of Christian Science was "higher, clearer, and more permanent than that given eighteen centuries ago." Joseph Smith, the Mormon prophet, claimed to be called by God to "restore" the Christian gospel which had been lost for eighteen centuries. And Charles and Myrtle Fillmore were self-appointed messiahs of the Unity School of Christianity's metaphysical maze. The syndrome of self-sanctification runs through the whole kingdom of the cults, and Mr. Armstrong is no exception. We are warned about such self-made "Christs" by Jesus in Matthew 24:24.

But has the Worldwide Church of God truly been consistent in its prophetic interpretations and its supernatural pronouncements since Mr. Armstrong first launched it? If Mr. Armstrong and his church really do speak for God, as they maintain, and if it is the only church that is preaching Christ's gospel, we have a right to expect that his Church will not deviate from that original gospel; but such is not the case.

The following examples of how Mr. Armstrong has changed his position over the last five decades offers ample proof of his fallibility and the emptiness of his claim to divine direction. It is one thing if a man says that he is speaking for himself; it is quite another to represent one's teachings as inspired by God, and as dependable in that most important field of biblical prophecy. If Mr. Armstrong is preaching Christ's gospel and God's Word, then let him hear what God has said: "I am the Lord; I do not change" (Mal. 3:6). Mr. Armstrong and his church's doctrines, however, *have* changed, and the following evidence is submitted as convincing proof.

The God That Failed

Three nineteen-year time cycles. In keeping with his almost superstitious fascination with numbers, HWA (Armstrong) used to be fond of drawing numerological parallels between the apostolic church and his own organization. Just as nineteen years passed between the Great Day of Pentecost and the penetration of Europe with the Gospel in A.D. 50, so nineteen years passed between the launching of the Armstrong "Work" in 1934 and the Armstrong gospel's "leap" of the Atlantic in 1953, when "The World Tomorrow" was broadcast to Europe via Radio Luxembourg. A second nineteen-year period ended with the destruction of Jerusalem and the flight of the remnant church to Pella in A.D. 69. Although he backed off from setting dates, especially toward the close of the cycle, Armstrong gave his followers the distinct impression that the "one true church" would be raptured to Petra, in the Jordanian wilderness south of the Dead Sea, and that the dreaded tribulation would commence on the thirty-eighth anniversary of his first regular broadcast, i.e., on January 7, 1972. But as the deadline approached and the endtime events did not materialize, Armstrong withdrew from circulation his booklet *1975 in Prophecy* (which predicted Christ's return in 1975, midway through the seven-year tribulation period), and the doctrines of 1972, Petra, and the nineteen-year time cycles went down the drain.[6]

One does not have to be a great student of either logic or theology to recognize that Mr. Armstrong completely fulfills what Moses had in mind when he spoke of false prophets. In the book of Deuteronomy, Moses pointed out that one could discover a false prophet by the simple fact that when he spoke in the name of the Lord the things did not come to pass. This is precisely what has occurred with Mr. Armstrong, who claims that his church has been the only voice of God on the earth since 1934. He therefore qualifies under the Mosaic classification, and should not be respected. The god that inspired Mr. Armstrong failed him, as the evidence shows; he has, therefore, not spoken as a servant of the Lord, nor as a minister of the gospel of Jesus Christ.

BASIC ERRORS IN THEOLOGY
The Trinity

The *purpose* of life is that in us God is really re-creating His *own kind—reproducing himself after His own kind*—for we are, upon real conversion, actually *begotten* as sons (yet unborn) of [God]; then, through study of God's revelation in His word, living by His every Word, constant prayer, daily experience with trials and testings, we grow spiritually more and more like God, until, at the time of the resurrection we shall be instantaneously *changed* from mortal into *immortal*—we shall then be *born [of God]—We shall then be God!*[7]

I suppose most people think of God as one single individual Person. Or, as a *"trinity." This is not true* . . . .

But the theologians and "Higher Critics" have blindly accepted the heretical and false doctrine introduced by *pagan* false prophets who crept in, that the *Holy Spirit* is a *third person*—the heresy of the *"trinity."* This *limits* God to "Three Persons."[8]

The Deity of Christ

Do you really grasp it? The *purpose* of your being alive is that finally you be *born* into the Kingdom of God, when you will actually *be* God, even as Jesus was and is God, and His Father, a different Person, also is God!

You are setting out on a training to become *creator*—to become God![9]

Yes, and as a born [son of God], Christ is God! God Almighty His Father is God. They are two separate and individual Persons (see Revelation 5:1,6,7).[10]

Jesus, alone, of all humans, has so far been saved! By the resurrective power of God! When Jesus comes, at the time of the resurrection of those in Christ, He then brings His reward with [Him]![11]

The Resurrection of Christ

When we are *born* [*of God*], *we shall be of His very family*—we shall be *spirit* as He is Spirit—immortal as He is immortal—divine as He is Divine![12]

Jesus Christ was *Dead* . . . —but was *revived!*
And the resurrected body was no longer human—it was the Christ resurrected, *immortal,* once again *changed!*[13]

If we overcome, grow in grace and knowledge and endure unto the end, *then* . . . this flesh and blood body, shall *become a spirit* body! Then, and not until then, shall we be *fully born* of God.

We are saved by *grace,* and through *faith* make no mistake about that; [*but*]—*there are conditions!*

It is only those who, during this Christian, Spirit-begotten life, have grown in knowledge and grace, have overcome, have developed spiritually, done the works of Christ, and endured unto the end, who shall finally be given *immortality*—finally changed from mortal to *immortal* at the time of the Second Coming of Christ (1 Corinthians 15:53-54).[14]

All true Christians who shall have died before Christ's coming shall rise first—in a resurrection—and then all Christians *still alive,* in mortal flesh, shall be instantaneously—in the twinkling of an eye—*changed* [*from mortal to*] *immortal*—from material flesh to immaterial *spirit*—from *human to divine,* at last *born* [*of*] *God!*[15]

We are now *flesh*—vile, corruptible flesh subject to rotting and decay. But at Christ's coming, when we shall be born [of God], this vile body shall be *changed,* and made exactly like Jesus in

His *glorified body!*[16]

The New Birth

But, He was then *born [of God], how?* By a resurrection from the dead (Romans 1:4). *When? At the time* of His resurrection!

And *that is* the way *you* and I shall look, if and when we are finally *born [of God]!* These deceived people who talk about having had a "born again experience" certainly don't look like *that!*

That tremendous, glorious event of being *born [of God]* is to take place *at the resurrection of the just*—at the time of Christ's Second Coming to earth![17]

Salvation by Grace

Salvation, then, *is a process!*

But how the god of this world would blind your eyes to that! He tries to deceive you into thinking all there is to it is just "accepting Christ" with "*no works*"—and presto-chango, you are pronounced "*Saved.*"

But the *Bible* reveals that *none* is yet saved![18]

People have been taught, falsely, that "Christ *completed* the plan of salvation on the Cross"— when actually it was only *begun* there. The popular denominations have taught, "Just *believe*— that's all there is to it; believe on the Lord Jesus Christ, and you are that instant *saved!*"

That teaching is false! And because of deception—because the *true Gospel* of Jesus Christ has been all but blotted out, lo these 1900 years by the preaching of a false gospel *about [the] person of Christ*—and often a false Christ at that—millions today *worship Christ—and all in vain!*

The blood of Christ does not finally save any man. The death of Christ did pay the penalty of sin in our stead—it wipes the slate clean of past sins—it saves us merely from the *death penalty*—it removes that which separated us from God and reconciles us to God.[19]

So it is not only *possible* but obligatory— that we obey God's spiritual law, *the ten commandments,* as they are magnified throughout the Bible. Keeping them in the spirit does *not mean* "spiritualizing" them away.

. . . But by exercising the *will* to always obey God, and by receiving the extra help He needed to master His fleshly desires, Jesus *repudiated* the sway of sin of the human flesh and showed that the law of God *could be kept.*[20]

Legalism, the Sabbath, and Unclean Foods

Passover, the days of unleavened bread, Pentecost, and the holy days God had ordained *forever* were all observed by Jesus . . . .

The New Testament reveals that Jesus, the apostles, and the New Testament Church, both Jewish and Gentile-born, observed God's Sabbaths, and God's festivals—weekly and annually![21]

It would be impossible in the light of the above and the limitations of space to answer all of Mr. Armstrong's mistakes in detail, but a biblical critique is vitally important if Christians are to protect themselves from the subtleties of his legalistic errors as well as to evangelize those within the Armstrong movement who are sincere but deceived. There is also a great mass of persons subjected to constant bombardment of Armstrong theology through the media who need to be warned that they are dealing with a theological wolf garbed in the clothing of an innocent lamb. Warning and exhortation are never popular in any age, but the Church has the task of doing both, and the facts must be presented and carefully weighed in the interest of truth.

TO EVERY MAN AN ANSWER

In the very beginning of this survey of the Worldwide Church of God I pointed out that Mr. Armstrong draws his theology from many sources, and then sprays on it a light veneer of Christian terminology combined with out-of-context quotations from the Bible. This tends to confuse people, many of whom are desperately seeking for truth and for some word from God to meet their needs. In the midst of all this are pious pronouncements from Mr. Armstrong, such as "Don't take my word for it—check it with the Bible." I intend to do just that now, and to find out if the Armstrong theology will stand up under the test of biblical revelation.

The Trinity

The Worldwide Church of God, as the preceding quotes reveal, rejects the Christian doctrine of the Trinity, teaching instead that the Trinity, or God's nature, is not limited to three Persons, but that actually the Trinity is a family concept in which all persons who accept Mr. Armstrong's religion will share! The Mormon church has taught for more than 140 years that through their priesthood a man may become *a god,* but Mr. Armstrong has surpassed them in that man may *become God.*

Biblical theology is most clear at this point, teaching that within the nature of the one eternal God there are three Persons—the Father, the Son, and the Holy Spirit (2 Pet. 1:17; Exod. 3:14; Rev. 1:11-18; John 1:1, 18; 8:58; Rev. 22:12-16; Col. 2:9; Titus 2:13; Acts 5:3-4; Isa. 45:22; 48:16). The Lord Jesus Christ commanded that the gospel be preached in all the world and that baptism be administered in the name of the Trinity, i.e., God (Matt. 28:19). Far from teaching that man may become God, the Scriptures teach that God forbids any such idea (Isa. 43:10), affirming instead that God is unique and one in essence (Deut. 6:4).

It is unnecessary to go any further into a refutation of Mr. Armstrong's views on the Trinity, since it has been documented from both Scripture and history that the Christian Church has always taught unity in Trinity and Trinity in unity, the full understanding of which God has reserved to Himself until the day when Christ will deliver up the kingdom to the Father, and God will be all in all (1 Cor. 15:28).

For further study and confirmation, consult the following texts:

1. Old Testament Hints—Genesis 1:26; 3:22; 11:7; Isaiah 6:8; 48:12; Zechariah 12:9-10.
2. The Creation—Genesis 1:2; John 1:3.
3. The Incarnation—Luke 1:35.
4. The Baptism of Christ—Matthew 3:16-17.
5. The Resurrection of Christ—Acts 3:26; 1 Thessalonians 1:10 (the Father); John 2:19-21 (the Son); Romans 8:11; 1 Peter 3:18 (the Holy Spirit); Acts 17:31 (God).
6. The Great Commission—Matthew 28:19.
7. The Divine Benediction—2 Corinthians 13:14. See also John 14:16, 26; 15:26.

The Deity of Christ

Perhaps the most famous of Garner Ted Armstrong's sermons, which was rebroadcast many times on television and radio, dealt with the identity of Jesus Christ. In this lengthy exposition, Garner Ted Armstrong affirmed that "Jesus is God," thus creating the impression that the Armstrong religion believes in the deity of Jesus Christ. As we have observed from his own published statements, Garner Armstrong and his father denied the unique deity of Jesus Christ, affirming that we can become God "just as Jesus is God . . . and His Father is God . . . . " New Testament theology specifically contradicts the Armstrongs at this point by declaring that Jesus Christ is Deity from all eternity (Rev. 1:7-8; John 1:1; Col. 2:9), whereas *man* is created in time and does not have an eternal past. For us to be God as Jesus is God, we would have to be eternal—but we are not (Gen. 1:26-27; 3:19,22).

Even to Old Testament scholars the deity of the Saviour was no secret, since he was termed by Isaiah "the father of eternity" (Isa. 9:6), whose heritage is from eternity (Mic. 5:2). In direct confrontation with the Jews of His day who were hostile to His messianic claims, Christ asserted the divine name as belonging to Him (John 8:58), and the Jews, understanding this claim, sought to stone Him for it (v. 59). Throughout His earthly ministry Jesus Christ accepted worship (Matt. 8:2; 14:33; John 9:35-39; 20:27-29) and allowed Thomas to proclaim Him the eternal God (John 20:28). In his Epistle to the Colossians, Paul describes Christ as the Creator of all things (1:16), and in Philippians 2 it is declared that He never ceased to be in the form of God (v. 6). Who can read the first chapter of the Epistle to the Hebrews without recognizing that Christ is the visible stamp of the divine nature in human flesh (v. 3), as well as the only one ever to be addressed by the Father, "Thy throne, O God, is for ever and ever" (v. 8). The genuine deity of Jesus Christ is the church's first affirmation—"He is Lord of all." God literally became flesh for us and our salvation (John 1:1, 14). Mr. Armstrong's error is the same error as that of the Sadducees, of whom Christ said, "You do err, not understanding the Scriptures nor the power of God" (see Mark 12:24).

The Resurrection of Christ

The Apostle Paul in his first Epistle to the Corinthians, chapter 15, adamantly and dogmatically taught that if Christ be not risen from the dead your faith is empty; you are still in your sins (v. 17).

Even a superficial reading of any Greek lexicon or dictionary would have told Mr. Armstrong that the word *resurrection* refers to the body, never to the soul or spirit, and this holds true in the Hebrew language as well. When the apostle was speaking, then, for him the term *risen,* the concept of the resurrection itself, involved the body and not the spirit. By teaching that Jesus Christ rose from the dead as a spirit without a physical form, Mr. Armstrong joins the Jehovah's Witnesses, the Dawn Bible Students, and countless liberal clergymen in the promulgation of an error first made by the disciples of our Lord, and corrected personally by Him! Luke informs us that Christ's disciples believed He was a spirit when they first saw Him after His resurrection, to which misconception Jesus responded: "Why are ye troubled? and why do thoughts arise in your hearts? Behold my hands and my feet, that it is I myself: handle me, and see; for a spirit hath not flesh and bones, as ye see me have" (Luke 24:38-39).

Mr. Armstrong stands contradicted out of the mouth of our Lord Himself, not to mention Luke and John. In the twentieth chapter of John's Gospel, Christ again affirmed the bodily nature of His resurrection (vv. 24-28), and in the one prophecy He gave concerning the nature of His resurrection body He vigorously affirmed it to be physical (John 2:19-21).

The final blow to the Armstrong myth that Christ was raised as a spirit is found in 1 John 3:2, where Christians are told that "it does not yet appear what we shall be, but we know that when he appears we shall be like him, for we shall see him as he is."

It is obvious from 1 Thessalonians chapter 4 that man emerges from the resurrection with a *physical form,* and that even in the resurrection of the unjust, they too will have physical forms (1 Thess. 4:13-17; Rev. 20:11-15).

Logic compels me to point out that if we are going to be like Christ in the resurrection and we are to receive resurrection bodies similar to His, He could hardly have been raised a spirit.

Since all hope for the Christian is grounded in the resurrection of the Lord Jesus, Mr. Armstrong with his denial of that resurrection attacks the cornerstone of the Christian faith, a faith he claims to support. Jesus said, "Wisdom is justified of her children." Let the wise student of Scripture understand that when Mr. Armstrong speaks of the resurrection of Christ, *his* Christ is a ghost; the *real* Jesus is a resurrected, immortal man.

The New Birth—A New Twist

The doctrine of the new birth or spiritual regeneration as it is taught in the New Testament apparently has an effect upon Mr. Armstrong which is little short of hysterical. In his pamphlet *Just What Do You Mean—Born Again?* he vigorously criticizes the Christian doctrine of regeneration (see preceding quotations on this subject), and in its place he substitutes what is by all odds one of the strangest doctrines in cultism. Through it he has quite literally given new birth a new twist!

According to the theology of the Worldwide Church of God, the doctrine of the new birth is divided into two areas. In the first, which takes place upon the acceptance of Jesus Christ as the Son of God, the believer is impregnated with the life of God through the Holy Spirit, which Mr. Armstrong terms "begetting." The second phase is the new birth itself, which, he informs us, takes place not at the moment of faith but at the resurrection of the body![22]

Mr. Armstrong strenuously maintains that it is "a universal error" to believe that when a person is converted, when he has fully repented and accepted Christ in faith, such a person is born again in the biblical sense. For Herbert Armstrong the original Greek word *gennao* is the pivot point of the controversy. Armstrong holds that, since the word can also be translated "beget" or "conceive," the translators of the Bible erred in not rendering the word consistently as "begotten" instead of "born," and this they did because they "did not themselves *understand* God's Plan . . . . The experience of conversion, in this life, is a *begettal*, a 'conception,' an 'impregnation,' but *not yet a birth!*"[23]

It is worthwhile to note in studying this particular phase of Mr. Armstrong's theology that his appeal to the Greek, which was meant to carry the convincing weight of scholastic authority, in reality becomes the proverbial albatross around his neck. Mr. Armstrong's contention that "the original Greek, in which the New Testament was written, has *only the one word for both meanings*"[24] is a most damaging remark, for any good lexicon reveals immediately that the Greek has at least four other terms to describe the idea of conception and birth

(*sullabousa, tiktei, apotelestheisa,* and *apokuei*), which
are translated variously as "conceive," "bring forth,"
"delivered," "born," "when finished," and "begat." One
need only study Luke 1:24, 36; 2:21; James 1:15, 18, and
numerous other passages, and he will come to the
immediate conclusion that Mr. Armstrong has no concept whatever of New Testament Greek. In fact, the
Greek language even has a term which describes preg-
nancy from conception to delivery!

The followers of Mr. Armstrong must settle for an
impregnation by the Spirit and a gestation period (their
entire lives!) before they can be born again. This new
birth is dependent upon keeping the commandments of
God and enduring to the end (in Mr. Armstrong's theology), a fact overlooked by some of his more zealous disciples.

The fact that the new birth has nothing to do with the
resurrection is demonstrated by the usage of the term by
the Apostle Peter, who reminds us that through faith in
the Lord Jesus Christ we have been "born again" (past
tense) "not of corruptible seed, but of incorruptible, by
the word of God, which liveth and abideth for ever" (1
Pet. 1:23).

The new birth in the New Testament is synonymous
with spiritual regeneration to eternal life, and the very
fact that Jesus Christ and the apostles described the
possessors of the new birth as "saved" decimates Mr.
Armstrong's contention that one must wait until the resurrection in order to be born again.

In his Epistle to the Ephesians the Apostle Paul is
clear in his declaration that "by grace you have been
saved through faith; and this is not your own doing, it is
the gift of God—not because of works, lest anyone
should boast" (Eph. 2:8, literal translation). Here is the
usage of the past tense in reference to Christians, an

instance which is amply supplemented throughout the New Testament by such passages as John 3:36; 5:24; 6:47; Romans 8:1; 1 Peter 1:18; 1 John 5:1,11-13,20.

Mr. Armstrong has no scholarly precedent for subdividing the new birth and attempting to attach it to the resurrection of the body, something which the Scripture nowhere does. His is a lame attempt to distort the basic meaning of *gennao* (which, incidentally, he himself admits is listed in the lexicon as "to be born, to bring forth, to be delivered of"). It is only one more indication of the limitations of his resources.

After reading Mr. Armstrong's statements, any serious student of the Bible wonders how anyone could take seriously his theological interpretations, for if there is one thing that the Bible *does* emphatically teach, it is the fact that salvation is *not* a process but an accomplished fact, based upon the *completed* sacrifice of Jesus Christ (Heb. 1:3; 9:26,28).

Regarding Mr. Armstrong's shocking statement to the effect that the blood of Christ does not finally save anyone, this is in direct contradiction of the words of the Apostle Peter, who taught that we have not been redeemed by anything corruptible but "with the precious blood of Christ" (1 Pet. 1:19). It should be noted that this is in the *past tense* as an accomplished fact, a teaching amplified in the book of Hebrews repeatedly. The writer of Hebrews tells us that by one offering He has perfected forever them that are sanctified and that by the will of God "we are sanctified through the offering of the body of Jesus Christ once for all" (see Heb. 10:14).

The Lord Jesus has not "entered into the holy places made with hands, which are the figures of the true; but into heaven itself, now to appear in the presence of God for us: . . . for then must he often have suffered since the foundation of the world: but now once in the end of the world hath he appeared to put away sin by the sacrifice of himself. And as it is appointed unto men once to die, but after this the judgment: so Christ was once offered to bear the sins of many; and unto them that look for him shall he appear the second time without sin unto salvation" (Heb. 9:24,26-28).

When Jesus Christ addressed Nicodemus (John 3) and spoke of the new birth, He connected this birth to the person of the Holy Spirit, whom the disciples received in the upper room (John 20) and whose power and presence were manifested at Pentecost (Acts 2). This has always been accepted in Christian theology for just what the Bible says it is—an instantaneous experience of spiritual cleansing and recreation synonymous with the exercise of saving faith in the person of Jesus Christ and through the agency of the grace of God (Acts 2:8-10; 16:31; Col. 1:13-14; Gal. 2:20; 1 Cor. 6:11,19; 2 Cor. 5:17).

The Apostle Paul instructs us that our salvation has been accomplished not by any efforts on our part, but by "the kindness and love of God our Saviour" (Titus 3:4-7). It is not something we must wait for until the resurrection; it is our *present possession* in Christ, totally separate from the immortality of the body, which is to be bestowed at the return of Christ and the resurrection of the body (1 Cor. 15:49-54; 1 John 3:2; Rom. 6:5).

It is all well and good if Mr. Armstrong's followers wish to make the new birth a process, as indeed they do with the doctrine of salvation, but we must be quick to point out that this is not the *Christian* doctrine of the new birth and is not consistent with the revelation of the Bible. Mr. Armstrong's new twist to the new birth is just that, and the Christian Church can ill afford to sit by in silence while the Worldwide Church of God propagates it as biblical theology.

Salvation by Grace

As the theology of Armstrongism does violence to
the true nature of the new birth, so also does it categorically deny the biblical doctrine of the atonement.

According to Mr. Armstrong:

> Salvation, then, *is a process!* But how the
> god of this world would blind your eyes to that!
> He tries to deceive you into thinking all there is to
> it is just "accepting Christ"—with *"no works,"*—
> and presto chango, you're pronounced *"Saved!"*
> ... But the *Bible* reveals that *none* is as yet
> "saved." ... People have been taught, falsely,
> that "Christ *completed* the plan of salvation on
> the Cross"—when actually it was only *begun*
> there. The popular denominations have taught,
> "Just *believe,* that's all there is to it; believe on
> the Lord Jesus Christ, and you are that instant
> *saved.*" That teaching is false! ... The *blood* of
> Christ does not finally save any man.[25]

Mr. Armstrong and his Worldwide Church of God
consistently ignore the fact that Christ "offered one sacrifice for sins for ever, [and] sat down on the right hand of
God ... Having therefore, brethren, boldness to enter
into the holiest by the blood of Jesus, by a new and living
way, which he hath consecrated for us, through the veil,
that is to say, his flesh; and having a high priest over the
house of God; let us draw near with a true heart in full
assurance of faith, having our hearts sprinkled from an
evil conscience and our bodies washed with pure water.
Let us hold fast the profession of our faith without waver-
ing; (for he is faithful that promised)" (Heb. 10:12,19-
23).

The Apostle Paul reiterates the completed nature of the atonement upon the cross when he deals with the subject in such passages as Ephesians 1:7, Colossians 1:20, and Romans 5:9. The Apostle John's reminder that God has provided for continual cleansing from sin (1 John 1:7,9) should only serve to strengthen Christians in the knowledge that Jesus Christ has indeed by the sacrifice of the cross "loosed us from our sins in His own blood" (Rev. 1:5, literal translation). This is a completed act, the benefits of which are shed abroad in the hearts of all true believers by the Holy Spirit. Nowhere does the Bible teach that the atonement of Christ is *yet* to be completed! This particular doctrine is drawn from the early writings of Seventh-Day Adventists, with whom, as we mentioned, Mr. Armstrong was associated at one time. It is to the credit of the Adventists that their organization has officially repudiated this position, maintaining that the atonement has already been completed.

Pauline theology makes clear the fact that in Jesus Christ God has determined to redeem men by sovereign grace, and the record still stands: "For what saith the scripture? Abraham believed God, and it was counted unto him for righteousness. Now to him that worketh is the reward not reckoned of grace, but of debt. But to him that worketh not, but believeth on him that justifieth the ungodly, his faith is counted for righteousness. Even as David also describeth the blessedness of the man, unto whom God imputeth righteousness without works, saying, blessed are they whose iniquities are forgiven, and whose sins are covered. Blessed is the man to whom the Lord will not impute sin" (Rom. 4:3-8).

The theology of the Worldwide Church of God in regard to the doctrine of salvation is refuted thoroughly by the Apostle Paul in his Epistle to the Galatians; when describing the purpose of the law of God, Paul points out that its primary function was to "lead us to Christ" that we might be justified by faith. The law was a pedagogue, a teacher, but it was finally and completely fulfilled in the person of Jesus Christ, who was incarnate love, as the universal, all-fulfilling principle which is implemented through grace, first toward God and then toward one's neighbor (see Rom. 13:8-11).

Mr. Armstrong attaches to salvation the requirement of "keeping the law and commandments of God." This can only be described as adding to the gospel of grace the condition of law-keeping, a first-century heresy scathingly denounced in the Galatian Epistle as "another gospel" by no less an authority on the law than the Apostle Paul himself (Gal. 1:8-9; 2:16,21).

If all law is fulfilled in love, as Christ and the apostles taught, then the insistence upon observance of the Ten Commandments (or, for that matter, the other 603 laws of Moses) on the part of Mr. Armstrong and his followers as a condition of salvation injects into the Christian Church what the apostles so successfully expelled (Matt. 22:36-40; Acts 15:24).

It is certainly true that no informed Christian believes in the destruction or setting aside of the laws of God, but there is a vast difference between the *abolition* of law and the *fulfillment* of law, which fulfillment Christ accomplished once for all on the cross (Rom. 3:31; 10:4).

Legalism, the Sabbath, and Unclean Foods

Inherent within the theological structure of the Worldwide Church of God, and stemming from Mr. Armstrong's perversion of the biblical doctrine of salvation, is his insistence (also borrowed from the Seventh-Day Adventists) that Christians abstain from specific types of food which he claims are "unclean."

No devoted follower of the Worldwide Church of God

will therefore eat pork, lobster, clams, shrimp, oysters, or any of the other prohibitions of the Mosaic system. They are, in effect, Orthodox Jews in this particular area of theology!

In his first Epistle to Timothy, the Apostle Paul recognized among the Gentiles the problem of so-called unclean foods and dealt with it in the following manner: "Now the Spirit speaketh expressly, that in the latter times some shall depart from the faith, giving heed to seducing spirits, and doctrines of devils; speaking lies in hypocrisy; having their conscience seared with a hot iron, forbidding to marry, and commanding to abstain from meats, which God hath created to be received with thanksgiving of them which believe and know the truth. For every creature of God is good, and nothing to be refused, if it be received with thanksgiving: for it is sanctified by the word of God and prayer" (1 Tim. 4:1-5).

Further comment on this particular subject is unnecessary in the light of the apostle's clear statement, but a reading of the fourteenth chapter of Romans reveals instantly that Christians are not to sit in judgment upon one another regarding days of worship or foods to be consumed. We are not to judge spirituality on the basis of diet or the observance of days. But in the Worldwide Church of God this is not true, for Mr. Armstrong does indeed sit in judgment upon all those who do not subscribe to his particular interpretation of dietary laws allegedly enforceable in this era of history.

Relative to the problem of Sabbath-keeping, Mr. Armstrong also derived this from the Seventh-Day Adventist denomination, but he has gone farther than the Adventists have ever even intimated.

The literature of the Worldwide Church of God insists upon the observance of the Jewish feast days, new moons, festivals, and sabbaths, all of which were dealt with fully and finally by the Apostle Paul in his Colossian Epistle:

"And you, being dead in your sins and the uncircumcision of your flesh, hath he quickened together with him, having forgiven you all trespasses; blotting out the handwriting of ordinances that was against us, which was contrary to us, and took it out of the way, nailing it to his cross; and having spoiled principalities and powers, he made a show of them openly, triumphing over them in it. Let no man therefore judge you in meat or in drink, or in respect of an holyday, or of the new moon, or of the sabbath days: which are a shadow of things to come; but the body is of Christ" (Col. 2:13-17).

When the preceding quotation from Paul is placed beside his counsel in Romans 14, the picture is transparently clear:

"Let not him that eateth despise him that eateth not; and let not him which eateth not judge him that eateth: for God hath received him. Who art thou that judgest another man's servant? to his own master he standeth or falleth. Yea, he shall be holden up; for God is able to make him stand. One man esteemeth one day above another: another esteemeth every day alike. Let every man be fully persuaded in his own mind . . . . But why dost thou judge thy brother? or why dost thou set at naught thy brother? for we shall all stand before the judgment seat of Christ . . . . Let us not therefore judge one another any more: but judge this rather, that no man put a stumblingblock or an occasion to fall in his brother's way. I know, and am persuaded by the Lord Jesus, that there is nothing unclean of itself: but to him that esteemeth any thing to be unclean, to him it is unclean . . . . For meat destroy not the work of God. All things indeed are pure; but it is evil for that man who eateth with offence. It is good neither to eat flesh, nor to drink wine, nor any thing whereby thy brother stumbleth, or is offended, or is made weak" (Rom. 14:3-5,10,13-14,20-21).

There is a memorable passage in the book of Acts where, when the Council of Jerusalem was in session concerning the problem of Jewish prohibitions on diet and practice as it affected the Gentile converts, the Apostle James once for all time dealt with the issue, a fact Mr. Armstrong seems content to ignore:

"Wherefore my sentence is, that we trouble not them which from among the Gentiles are turned to God: but that we write unto them, that they abstain from pollutions of idols, and from fornication, and from things strangled, and from blood . . . . Forasmuch as we have heard, that certain which went out from us have troubled you with words, subverting your souls, saying, Ye must be circumcised, and keep the law: to whom we gave no such commandment: . . . For it seemed good to the Holy Ghost, and to us, to lay upon you no greater burden than these necessary things; that ye abstain from meats offered to idols, and from blood, and from things strangled, and from fornication: from which if ye keep yourselves, ye shall do well" (Acts 15:19-20,24,28-29).

It is evident that law-keeping, dietary prohibitions, the Mosaic ordinances which were binding upon Israel, and the Jewish customs of observances of feasts, etc., were abrogated by the Holy Spirit (v. 28), and it is certainly not amiss to comment that what the Spirit of God saw fit to lift as restrictions upon the Church of Jesus Christ, the so-called Worldwide Church of God has no right to reimpose! Mr. Armstrong, however, has done precisely this, and his action stands condemned not only by the Council at Jerusalem and the Apostle James, but by the clear words of the Apostle Paul and the pronouncement of the Holy Spirit Himself.

From our survey of the Worldwide Church of God it is apparent that the errors of Mr. Armstrong's religion place him well outside the pale of historic Christianity, and very definitely within the category of non-Christian cultism.

There are many sincere and devoted truth-seekers within the Armstrong cult, many of whom have been gleaned from liberal Protestantism and Catholicism, and who are attracted by Mr. Armstrong's emphasis upon the Bible, perverted though it may be. I have no doubt that there are people within the structure of the Armstrong religion who have a simple faith in Jesus Christ from their past experience and have simply been confused by Armstrong's dogmatic pronouncements in the name of God. The Apostle Paul told us of such persons in need of reclamation in 2 Corinthians 11:3-4: "But I fear, lest by any means, as the serpent beguiled Eve through his subtilty, so your minds should be corrupted from the simplicity that is in Christ. For if he that cometh preacheth another Jesus, whom we have not preached, or if ye receive another spirit, which ye have not received, or another gospel, which ye have not accepted, ye might well bear with him."

Let us take the words of the apostle seriously, believing that the followers of Mr. Armstrong have indeed been deceived by a counterfeit Christ, a counterfeit Holy Spirit, and a counterfeit gospel; and let us reach out to them, answering their questions and extending the love of Christ, so that they may "be reconciled to God" (2 Cor. 5:20). This is the task of the Church; this is the only effective answer to the rise of the cults.

NOTES

1. We asked Don Ricker of Armstrong's *Worldwide Advertising* for exact figures, but he declined to give us statistics.

2. Personal letter to Robert Sumner, November 27, 1958.

3. *Easter Is Pagan*, pp. 8-9.

4. *The Inside Story of the World of Tomorrow Broadcast*, pp. 7-11.

5. *Ibid.*, p. 4.

6. *Christianity Today*, April 15, 1977. Personal interview with Garner Ted Armstrong reported by Joseph Martin Hopkins, an authority on the Armstrong cult.

7. *Why Were You Born?* pp. 21-22.

8. *Just What Do You Mean—Born Again?* (Pasadena, CA: Ambassador College Press, 1963), pp. 17,19.

9. *Why Were You Born?* pp. 21-22.

10. *Just What Do You Mean—Born Again?* p. 16.

11. *Why Were You Born?* p. 12.

12. *Just What Do You Mean*, p. 15.

13. *The Plain Truth*, April 1963, p. 10.

14. *All About Water Baptism*, pp. 1,3.

15. *Just What Do You Mean*, pp. 14-15.

16. *Ibid.*, p. 13.

17. *Ibid.*

18. *Why Were You Born?* p. 11.

19. *All About Water Baptism*, p. 6.

20. *The Plain Truth*, November, 1963, pp. 11-12.

21. *Easter Is Pagan*, pp. 4,12.

22. *Just What Do You Mean*, pp. 6-7.

23. *Ibid.*, pp. 7-8.

24. *Ibid.*, p. 7.

25. *Why Were You Born?* p. 11; *All About Water Baptism*, p. 6.

For Further Reading

General References

Adair, James R. and Ted Miller, eds., *We Found Our Way Out,* Grand Rapids, MI: Baker Book House, 1964.

Bjornstad, James, *Counterfeits at Your Door,* Ventura, CA: Regal Books (Gospel Light Publications), 1979.

Boa, Kenneth, *Cults, World Religions and You,* Wheaton, IL: Victor Books (Scripture Press Publications), 1977.

Enroth, Ron, *The Lure of the Cults,* Chappaqua, NY: Christian Herald Books, 1979.

——— , *Youth, Brainwashing and Extremist Cults,*

Grand Rapids, MI: Zondervan Publishing Company, 1977.

_____ , and others, *A Guide to Cults and New Religions,* Downers Grove, IL: InterVarsity Press, 1983.

Gruss, Edmond C., *Cults and the Occult in the Age of Aquarius,* Nutley, NJ: Presbyterian and Reformed Publishing Company, 1974.

Hefley, James C., *The Youthnappers,* Wheaton, IL: Victor Books, 1977.

Hoekema, Anthony A., *The Four Major Cults,* Grand Rapids, MI: William B. Eerdmans Publishing Company, 1963.

Hunt, Dave, *The Cult Explosion,* Eugene, OR: Harvest House Publishers, 1980.

Larson, Bob, *Larson's Book of Cults,* Wheaton, IL: Tyndale House Publishers, 1982.

Lewis, Gordon R., *Confronting the Cults,* Grand Rapids, MI: Baker Book House, 1966.

Martin, Walter R., *The Kingdom of the Cults,* Minneapolis, MN: Bethany Book Publishers, 1965, 1975.

_____ , *The New Cults,* Ventura, CA: Vision House Publishers (Gospel Light Publications), 1980.

_____ , *The Rise of the Cults,* Ventura, CA: Vision House Publishers (Gospel Light Publications), 1980.

_____ , *Walter Martin's Cults Reference Bible,* Ventura, CA: Vision House Publishers (Gospel Light Publications), 1981.

Needleman, Jacob, *The New Religions,* New York, NY: E. P. Dutton and Company Inc., 1970.

Passantino, Robert and Gretchen, *Answers to the Cultist at Your Door,* Eugene, OR: Harvest House Publishers, 1981.

Peterson, William J., *Those Curious New Cults,* New Canaan, CT: Keats Publishers Inc., 1973, 1975.

Ridenour, Fritz, *So What's the Difference?,* Ventura, CA: Regal Books (Gospel Light Publications), 1967.

Rosten, Leo, ed., *Religions in America,* New York, NY: Simon and Schuster, 1962, 1963.

Sire, James W., *Scripture Twisting: Twenty Ways the Cults Misread the Bible,* Downers Grove, IL: InterVarsity Press, 1980.

Spittler, Russel P., *Cults and Isms: Twenty Alternatives to Evangelical Christianity,* Grand Rapids, MI: Baker Book House, 1962.

Stoner, Carroll and Jo Anne Parke, *All God's Children,* Radnor, PA: Chilton Book Company, 1977.

Van Baalen, J.K., *Chaos of the Cults,* Grand Rapids, MI: Eerdmans Publishing Company, 1962.

Jehovah's Witnesses

Countess, Robert H., *The Jehovah's Witnesses' New Testament,* Phillipsburg, NJ: Presbyterian and Reformed Publishing Company, 1982.

Dencher, Ted, *Why I Left Jehovah's Witnesses,* Fort Washington, PA: Christian Literature Crusade, 1966.

Gruss, Edmond C., *Apostles of Denial,* Nutley, NJ: Presbyterian and Reformed Publishing Company, 1970.

_____ , *The Jehovah's Witnesses and Prophetic Speculation,* Nutley, NJ: Presbyterian and Reformed Publishing Company, 1972.

_____ , ed., *We Left Jehovah's Witnesses: A Non-Prophet Organization,* Nutley, NJ: Presbyterian and Reformed Publishing Company, 1974.

Hoekema, Anthony A., *Jehovah's Witnesses,* Grand Rapids, MI: William B. Eerdmans Publishing Company, 1963.

Martin, Walter R., *Jehovah of the Watchtower,* Minneapolis, MN: Bethany Book Publishers, 1982.

_____ , *Jehovah's Witnesses,* Minneapolis, MN: Bethany Book Publishers, 1970.

Bergman, Jerry, *Jehovah's Witnesses and Blood Transfusions,* Costa Mesa, CA: CARIS, 1979.

_____ , *Jehovah's Witnesses and Mental Illness,* Costa Mesa, CA: CARIS, 1983.

Thomas, F.W., *Masters of Deception: An Exposé of the Jehovah's Witnesses,* Grand Rapids, MI: Baker Book House, 1970.

Van Buskirk, Michael, *The Scholastic Dishonesty of the Watchtower,* Costa Mesa, CA: CARIS, 1976.

Mormonism

Anderson, Einar, *The Inside Story of Mormonism,* Grand Rapids, MI: Kregel Publications, 1973, 1974.

Cowan, Marvin W., *Mormon Claims Answered,* Salt Lake City, UT: Marvin Cowan Publisher, 1975.

Cowdrey, Davis, and Scales with Gretchen Passantino, *Who Really Wrote the Book of Mormon?,* Ventura, CA: Vision House Publishers Inc., 1977, 1980.

Fraser, Gordon, *Is Mormonism Christian?,* Chicago, IL: Moody Press, 1957, 1977.

_____ , *Sects of the Church of the Latter-Day Saints,* Eugene, OR: Industrial Litho Incorporated, 1978.

Hoekema, Anthony, *Mormonism,* Grand Rapids, MI: William B. Eerdmans Publishing Company, 1963.

Martin, Walter R., *The Maze of Mormonism,* Ventura, CA: Vision House Publishers Inc., 1978.

_____ , *Mormonism,* Minneapolis, MN: Bethany Book House, 1963.

McElveen, Floyd C., *The Mormon Illusion,* Ventura, CA: Regal Books, 1977.

Ropp, Harry L., *The Mormon Papers: Are the Mormon Scriptures Reliable?,* Downers Grove, IL: InterVarsity Press, 1977.

Tanner, Jerald and Sandra, *The Changing World of Mormonism,* Chicago, IL: Moody Press, 1980.

_____ , *Mormonism: Shadow or Reality?,* Salt Lake City, UT: Modern Microfilm Company, 1972.

_____ , *3,913 Changes in the Book of Mormon,* Salt Lake City, UT: Modern Microfilm Company, n.d.

The Mind Sciences

Beals, Anne, *Crisis in the Christian Science Church,* Pasadena, CA: Ann Beals, 1978.

Beasley, Norman, *The Cross and the Crown: The History of Christian Science,* New York, NY: Duell, Sloan and Pearce, 1952.

Braden, Charles S., *Christian Science Today,* Dallas, TX: Southern Methodist University Press, 1958.

Dresser, Horatio W., ed., *The Quimby Manuscripts,* Secaucus, NJ: The Citadel Press, 1961.

Hoekema, Anthony, *Christian Science,* Grand Rapids, MI: William B. Eerdmans Publishing Company, 1963.

Martin, Walter R., *Christian Science,* Minneapolis, MN: Bethany Book House, 1963.

Milmine, Georgine, *The Life of Mary Baker G. Eddy and the History of Christian Science,* Grand Rapids, MI: Baker Book House, copyright 1909 by Doubleday, reprinted 1971 by Baker Books.

Peel, Robert, *Mary Baker Eddy,* New York, NY: Holt, Rinehart and Winston, 1966.

Powell, Lyman P., *Mary Baker Eddy,* New York, NY: The Macmillan Company, 1930.

The Occult

Adam, Ben, *Astrology: The Ancient Conspiracy,* Minneapolis, MN: Bethany Book House, 1963.

Bjornstad, James and Shildes Johnson, *Stars, Signs, and Salvation in the Age of Aquarius,* Minneapolis, MN: Bethany Book House, 1971.

Gasson, Raphael, *The Challenging Counterfeit,* Plainfield, NJ: Logos Books, 1966.

Gruss, Edmond, *Cults and the Occult in the Age of Aquarius,* Nutley, NJ: Presbyterian and Reformed Publishing Company, 1974.

Houdini, Harry and Joseph Dunninger, *Magic and Mystery: The Incredible Psychic Investigations of Houdini and Dunninger,* New York, NY: Weathervane Books, 1967.

Keen, M. Lamar with Allen Spraggett, *The Psychic Mafia: The True and Shocking Confessions of a Famous Medium,* New York, NY: St. Martin's Press, 1976.

Koch, Kurt, *Between Christ and Satan,* Grand Rapids, MI: Kregel Publications, 1962.

Korem, Danny and Paul Meier, *The Fakers,* Grand Rapids, MI: Baker Book House, 1980.

McDowell, Josh and Don Stewart, *Understanding the Occult,* San Bernardino, CA: Here's Life Publishers, 1982.

Michaelson, Johanna, *The Beautiful Side of Evil,* Eugene, OR: Harvest House Publishers, 1982.

Noorbergen, Rene, *The Soul Hustlers,* Grand Rapids, MI: Zondervan Publishing House, 1976.

Spence, Lewis, *An Encyclopedia of Occultism,* Secaucus, NJ: The Citadel Press, 1960.

Stemman, Roy, *One Hundred Years of Spiritualism,* London: Spiritualist Association of Great Britain, 1972.

Weldon, John and Zola Levitt, *Psychic Healing,* Chicago, IL: Moody Press, 1982.

Wilson, Clifford and John Weldon, *Occult Shock and Psychic Forces,* San Diego, CA: Master Books, 1980.

The New Cults

Bjornstad, James, *The Moon Is Not the Sun,* Minneapolis, MN: Bethany Book House, 1976.

Boa, Kenneth, *Cults, World Religions, and You,* Wheaton, IL: Victor Books, 1977.

Edwards, Christopher, *Crazy for God: The Nightmare of Cult Life,* Englewood Cliffs, NJ: Prentiss Hall, Inc., 1979.

Elkins, Chris, *Heavenly Deception,* Wheaton, IL: Tyndale House Publishers, Inc., 1980.

Enroth, Ronald, *The Lure of the Cults,* Chappaqua, NY: Christian Herald Books, 1979.

_____ , *Youth, Brainwashing and the Extremist Cults,* Grand Rapids, MI: Zondervan Publishing House, 1977.

Evans, Christopher, *The Cults of Unreason,* New York, NY: Dell Publishing Company, Inc., 1973.

Hefley, James C., *The Youthnappers,* Wheaton, IL: Scripture Press Publications, 1977.

Kemperman, Steve, *Lord of the Second Advent: A Rare Look Inside the Terrifying World of the Moonies,* Ventura, CA: Regal Books, 1981.

Lewis, Gordon R., *What Everyone Should Know About Transcendental Meditation,* Ventura, CA: Regal Books, 1975.

Martin, Walter R., *The New Cults,* Ventura, CA: Vision House Publishers, Inc., 1980.

_____ , *Walter Martin's Cults Reference Bible,* Ventura, CA: Vision House Publishers, Inc., 1982.

Miller, Calvin, *Transcendental Hesitation,* Grand Rapids, MI: Zondervan Publishing House, 1977.

Needleman, Jacob, *The New Religions,* New York, NY: E. P. Dutton and Company, Inc., 1970.

Passantino, Robert and Gretchen, *Answers to the Cultist at Your Door,* Eugene, OR: Harvest House Publishers, 1981.

Peterson, William J., *Those Curious New Cults,* New Canaan, CT: Keats Publishers Inc., 1973, 1975.

Sire, James W., *Scripture Twisting: Twenty Ways the Cults Misread the Bible,* Downers Grove, IL: InterVarsity Press, 1980.

White, Mel, *Deceived,* Old Tappan, NJ: Fleming H. Revell Company, 1979.

Williams, J.L., *Victor Paul Wierwille and The Way International,* Chicago, IL: Moody Press, 1979.

Yamamoto, J. Isamu, *The Puppet Master,* Downers Grove, IL: InterVarsity Press, 1977.